HIDDEN
HEADLINES
OF
NEW YORK

**Strange, Unusual, & Bizarre Newspaper Stories
1860-1910**

HIDDEN HEADLINES
OF
NEW YORK

Strange, Unusual, & Bizarre Newspaper Stories
1860-1910

Researched and Compiled by
Chad Lewis

UNEXPLAINED
Research Publishing Company
A Division of Unexplained Research, LLC

Library of Congress Control Number: 2007928697
ISBN-10: 0-9762099-9-3
ISBN-13: 978-0-9762099-9-7

Printed in the United States by Documation

Unexplained Research Publishing Company
A Division of Unexplained Research LLC
P.O. Box 2173, Eau Claire, WI 54702-2173
Email: info@unexplainedresearch.com
www.unexplainedresearch.com

Cover Design: Jeannine & Terry Fisk
Illustrations: Rick Fisk
Portrait: Rob Mattison

DEDICATION

This book is dedicated to **Nathan Lewis**,
whose quick-wittedness would certainly put him in good graces with
the people of New York.

TABLE OF CONTENTS

"Keep Your Powder Dry"
—Bill "Willie" Lewis

Introduction

They say New Yorkers have seen and heard everything, and that may indeed be true, but I guarantee you that unless a person is 160 years old, they have not seen these bizarre stories. But don't take my word for it . . . go ahead and stop someone in downtown New York City and ask them if they are familiar with the half human-half monkey that came into port, or pull into a small rural town and inquire if they know where the sea serpent was spotted in 1875. On second thought, you may just want to trust me, because if you ask too many people about the man with the celluloid nose you may just end up in the insane asylum like a few of the unfortunate souls in this book did.

Go ahead and think back to the 1800s. What thoughts spring forth to your mind? When we look back at the1800s and think of how people lived, worked, traveled, and played, it seems like they were living in a completely different world than what we are familiar with today. We often believe that those who lived 100 years ago were well-grounded, rational, more conservative, and possessed greater common sense than we do today. Their world moved at a slower pace, seemed less chaotic, and provided time to reflect on the important issues of the day.

Unfortunately, the good old days are gone, and no wishing will ever bring them back. Yet these stories provide a rare opportunity to vicariously experience what it was like to be a resident in early New York. Allow yourself to be transported back to a time long since past, but be prepared—the newspapers of old were not quite like those of today. The style of writing, along with the spattering of aged words may appear a bit old fashioned and archaic to you, but if you let it this "old" type of writing will make you feel like you just picked today's newspaper off your front porch. Readers may also be shocked by some of the language that is outright sexist, racist, and bigoted. To accurately present these stories in their historical context, I have not censored or changed any of the writing or wording.

Robert Ripley, the great chronicler of the weird, spent his life traveling to exotic locations in search of the mysterious and unknown. He brought back amazing stories and priceless artifacts for the nation to gaze upon in complete wonder. However, Ripley wisely knew that the weird wasn't exclusively harbored in the remote corners of the planet; he believed that some of the most bizarre stories and people lived right here with us, right in our own backyards. Well, I grabbed the shovel and started digging these stories up, and what I found will hopefully prove Mr. Ripley right.

Regardless of what conclusions you come to after reading this book, I am certain that these New York stories will provide you a glimpse of the state in its simpler, slower-paced, and much, much weirder past.

Enjoy the adventure,
Chad Lewis

ACKNOWLEDGMENTS

I would like to thank Nisa Giaquinto, Sarah Szymanski, Rob Mattison, Rick Fisk, Jeannine Fisk, and Terry Fisk for assisting with the research and production of this book.

Singular Coincidence
Death Of Two Prominent Men Of Troy While Their Wives Were On A Picnic

TROY- William Madden, a prominent citizen, Past Grand Master of the State lodge of Odd Fellows, died this morning of apoplexy. Coroner C. S. Woodruff, a prominent homeopathic physician died this afternoon, the result of an overdose of mandrake taken to relieve pains. Mrs. Madden and Mrs. Woodruff are on an excursion to the Catskills, beyond telegraphic communication.

—Port Jervis Evening Gazette
July 1, 1880

Died In A Cemetery

LANSINGBURGH- George Scott, a prominent manufacturer of Lansingburgh, dropped dead while arranging a lot in Oakwood Cemetery to-day. He was the Prohibition candidate for Assembly in the second District of Rensselaer County in the late elections.

—New York Times
December 4, 1884

Lansingburgh was named after its founder, Abraham Jacob Lansing.

Died In Cemetery
Mrs. Justina Bukowski Dropped Dead At Oakwood Cemetery This Morning

SYRACUSE- Mrs. Justina Bukowski of No. 143 Steuben Street dropped dead in Oakwood Cemetery, where she was employed, at about 7 o'clock this morning. She had been a sufferer from heart trouble. She was 62 years old and leaves a family. The remains were taken to Burns & Gayner's rooms, and later to those of Undertaker Wenz.

—Syracuse Evening Herald
October 1, 1898

Man And Wife Die While Walking Home
She Succumbs To Heart Disease And Apoplexy Immediately Carries Him Off

BROOKLYN- Emil Reuter, a wholesale flour dealer of Brooklyn, and his wife Ida died last night. They had attended a theater and were on the way home when Mrs. Reuter fell to the sidewalk. She was carried into the house in front of which she had fallen and doctors were called, but Mrs. Reuter was dead when they arrived. Reuter left to tell a friend of his wife's death and was re-entering the house in which her body lay when he was suddenly stricken down. Mrs. Reuter's death was caused by heart disease and her husband of apoplexy.

—Milwaukee Journal
January 27, 1899

The first pizzeria was established in New York City in 1895.

HIDDEN HEADLINES of NEW YORK

Woman Burned To Death

By A Strange Coincidence Her Husband Suffered A Serious Accident At The Same Time

OGDENSBURG- While Mrs. Hugh Beggs, who kept a boarding house for canal workmen, was preparing breakfast to-day a lamp exploded setting fire to her clothes. She ran from the house to the barn, setting fire to it. The woman died of her injuries. About the same time Mr. Beggs had a fall upon some works on the canal and broke five of his ribs.

—*Syracuse Post Standard*
July 15, 1899

EXTRA! EXTRA!

Ogdensburg is the home of the Robert C. McEwen Customs House, the oldest federally-owned building in the U.S.

The Deadly Toy Pistol

MANHATTAN- William McNulty, 12 years old, of No. 256 West One Hundred and Fifteenth Street, who was taken to the Manhattan hospital yesterday, died there yesterday morning. He shot himself in the first finger of the left hand with a blank cartridge on the Fourth, tearing away a part of the finger. He was treated at home until yesterday. The physicians injected some of the tetanus serum into McNulty's breast Wednesday afternoon and under its influence the boy seemed to improve to such a degree that it was decided to inject the serum into his brain yesterday. He became mysteriously worse during the night.

Joseph Rezhofsky, 13 years old, of Blondell Avenue, Westchester, died as a result of a pistol shot wound of the hand. Joseph Fries, 12 years old, of East Chester Road, Westchester, was taken to the Morrisania police court yesterday morning on suspicion of having shot Rezhofsky. Frank Rezhofsky, 7 years old, a brother of the dead boy, declared that Fries had accidentally shot his brother with a blank cartridge. Another boy said that Rezhofsky had shot himself, and declared that he saw the accident. Magistrate Flammer paroled Fries until Tuesday.

Rezhofsky's mother put tea leaves on the wound after the accident and kept the boy at home. Yesterday she called in a doctor. He said she had waited too long, and that lockjaw had set in. He tried to help the little fellow, but could not, and Rezhofsky died in fearful agony. Joseph Lavinsky, another victim of tetanus, died at Bellevue Hospital at 2:30 o'clock yesterday morning. His skull had been trephined on Wednesday night and the anti-toxin injected into the brain, but the treatment was not successful. Martin Breen, 10 years old, of No. 197 North First Street, Paterson, died of lockjaw yesterday. On the Fourth Breen and some companions secured a small canon and fired it in the open lots near their homes. Once the gun exploded prematurely, the ramrod being driven into Breen's leg. The boy was placed in charge of a physician and the wound healed rapidly.

Yesterday, however, tetanus set in and Breen died yesterday morning before the arrangements could be completed for the application of the new serum treatment. The presumption is that the ramrod was rusty and that the dread tetanus bacilli thus found their way into Breen's blood. Gustav Salinski lost his life by a firecracker exploding in his hand, which led to lockjaw. He was 16 years old and his home was in Yonkers. He died in St. John's Hospital early yesterday morning. His wound, unlike those in most of the cases now attracting notice, had not healed.

Fred Grisbach of Monowesee, near New Haven, Conn., went for a week without medical attendance for his wounded hand because his parents were too poor. He received the charge from a toy pistol on the Fourth of July and his hand became more and more inflamed. Dr. Goodyear found the lad suffering from a deadly attack of lockjaw. Within two days after the physician was called little Grisbach died, after undergoing terrible agonies. He was 14 years old, and was the son of Herman Grisbach, a former fireman, who for months has been too ill to work.

Charles R. Broadhead, 13 years old, son of Daniel D. Broadhead of No. 16 La Tourette Avenue, Bayonne, died late Wednesday night at the City hospital there. The child had received a troublesome wound in the hand. A splinter from a blank cartridge had lodged in the flesh. The wound healed over, and little more was thought of it until Wednesday morning, when the disease became manifest. Convulsions set in quickly and he died in a spasm of pain.

Edward Minchell, a 14-year-old boy, died at No. 906 East Washington Street, Syracuse, N.Y., yesterday from lockjaw, which was caused by an injury to his hand. He was shot with a toy pistol on July 4th.

—*Dallas Morning News*
July 22, 1899

His Good Fortune
Was His Undoing
Starving Man Found Money,
Bought Food And
Choked To Death.

NEW YORK- An unknown and starving man found a $2 bill to-day, went to a Park Row restaurant, ordered a large portion of roast and was chocked to death by a piece of the meat despite the efforts of a surgeon. Nothing by which to identify the man was found.

—*Syracuse Post Standard*
January 5, 1900

Frightened To Death
Little Girl Dropped Dead
When She Saw A Peddler

GOWANDA- Eva Harris, the 10-year-old daughter of E. L. Harris of this village, dropped dead from fright yesterday afternoon. The little girl was playing on the sidewalk in front of her home when an Italian peddler came along. The child looked up, saw the peddler coming towards as if to speak to her, gave a piercing scream and fell dead at the man's feet.

The child's mother rushed from the house as she heard little Eva's scream, but the child was dead before her mother reached her side. The peddler was arrested and will be held pending an investigation by the Coroner. He says that he is innocent of any intention of injuring the child and that he does not know why she was frightened. The little girl's parents say that she had always been very much afraid of tramps and peddlers, especially those carrying packs, as the man who frightened her to death yesterday did. She also had heart trouble.

—*Syracuse Evening Herald*
February 13, 1900

Accusation
Killed A Friend

SEWARD- Because he was asked to search the books at the Post Office over which his life-long friend presided, for evidences of embezzlement, S. J. Figgard was so shocked that he dropped dead. For many days Post Office secret service men have been watching Postmaster Simmons. To-day they concluded there was sufficient evidence of crookedness to place the bondsmen in charge of the office and did so.

To ascertain the situation, the officers called on Figgard, an expert accountant, and requested that he go over the books. He was standing on the street corner when approached. He observed: "Why yes I will go over the books for you, but what is wrong?" When told that it was feared Simmons was short in his accounts, Figgard suddenly said: "Oh surly not, he is an honest man." Then he fell forward on his face. When picked up he was dead.

Later the officers found what they considered evidence that Simmons was an embezzler to the extent of $3,000. He was taken to Lincoln to-night. Figgard and Simmons were lifelong friends. Both men are prominent in State politics. Simmons was a warm friend of Senator Thurston and was appointed on his recommendation.

—*New York Times*
February 17, 1900

**EXTRA!
EXTRA!**

Four Presidents of the United States were born in New York. They are Martin Van Buren, Millard Fillmore, Theodore Roosevelt, and Franklin Delano Roosevelt.

Frightened To Death
A Giant Skeleton Rigged Up On Wires Causes A Young Girl To Drop Dead

KARRDALE- The authorities of Allegheny County are looking for the persons who manufactured a skeleton out of animals' bones which frightened Mary Oldfield of Karrdale to death Wednesday night. Miss Oldfield, accompanied by two friends, was returning from a Halloween party, where they had listened to gruesome stories until their hair stood on ends.

When about to enter the woods, a rattling of bones was heard overhead and, looking up, the trio were overcome with horror at seeing a skeleton of gigantic proportions sweeping down on them from above. With a cry of horror, Mary dropped dead. A searching party found a wire leading from the ground to a treetop, to which was attached a skeleton by a pulley.

—*Dallas Morning News*
November 3, 1900

Dropped Dead
While Dancing
Rapdorf Was His Wife's Partner In A Two-step At A Church Social

BROOKLYN- While dancing a two-step last night with his wife at a social entertainment given in connection with his church, Richard Rapdorf of Bradford Street near Glenmore Avenue, Brooklyn, fell dead. The entertainment was being given at Turn Hall, which is in the vicinity of the Rapdorf residence and was under the auspices of the Vigilant Social Club, and organization connected with the Wyona Street Lutheran Church.

Although it was Sunday night, a lively two-step was being enjoyed by a majority of the couples present, and none was following the music with keener enjoyment than the Rapdorfs, husband and wife. Suddenly Rapdorf let go of his wife and sank to the floor. An ambulance was summoned, but the surgeon said that the man had died instantly of heart disease.

—*New York Times*
November 15, 1900

Dropped Dead
At Her Surprise Party

FISHKILL LANDING- Miss Josephine Keating, aged thirty-five years, of New London, Conn., dropped dead at the close of a surprise party given in her honor here last night. She was tendered the party at the home of her cousin, James Hayes, and at midnight, just after supper, she threw up her hands and expired. She intended to leave for her home in New London, to-day. Coroner Goring will hold an inquest, to-morrow.

—*New York Times*
February 9, 1901

EXTRA! EXTRA!

Fishkill Landing, what a wonderfully unique name, unfortunately the town's name has been changed to Beacon.

Died Before His Wife Did
**Husband Who Said He Would Go
Before Her,
Stricken As She Lay Dying.**

NEW YORK- "I will die before you do, Margaret." This had been the burden of Edward Phelan's speech during the five years of his wife's invalidism. "I would not care to live after you are gone, and I know you would not be satisfied to go and leave me here after all these years."

His words were prophetic, although up to Tuesday morning, when he died, he was a strong, robust man, who carried his sixty-nine years with ease, and who might have been taken for a man in middle life by the casual observer. But the couple were not long separated—less than twenty-four hours later Mrs. Phelan, who had long been marked for death, breathed her last.

Forty-seven years ago Edward Phelan and his bride left the old home in Ireland and came to America to better their fortunes, and, while they never accumulated any very large amount if this world's goods, they lived happily in New York and never knew what it was to want for the comforts of life.

Children came, grew up, and married off all but one, a daughter, who remained with the old folks to the end. About five years ago Mrs. Phelan's health began to fail and recently she declined rapidly. Her husband had devoted most of his time to nursing her, but as it was a labor of love, the task did not tell at all upon him. He kept his health and his spirits. One way he had of cheering his wife was to say that she was stronger than he, or, at least that she would survive him. But to this she would only smile and say that if it was the Lord's will she was content to go first.

Within the last two weeks a change, decidedly for the worse, set in, and it became apparent that the end was near. Mr. Phelan realized this, and at their home, 20 Rector Street, he was a constant attendant at her bedside. Tuesday morning the doctors and attendants told him she was dying. For the first time since he slipped the wedding ring on her finger in far-off Ireland she failed to respond to his hand pressure. Up to that time he had been brave and hopeful, but the shock was more than he could bear. He retired to an adjoining room and within a few minutes was in a complete state of collapse. Three hours later he was dead.

The wife never heard of it. She passed away at 8:45 Wednesday morning without

HIDDEN HEADLINES of NEW YORK

regaining consciousness. Only two children survive the couple, a son, who is a clerk, and a daughter, who lived at home with her parents. Last night the home was crowded by sympathizing friends, all of whom united in the opinion that Edward Phelan had died of a broken heart. Husband and wife will be buried in one grave to-day.

—*New York Times*
July 5, 1901

Mother And Daughter Buried Together
Williamsburg. A Double Funeral Took Place Yesterday From 306 Walworth Street.

WILLIAMSBURG- It was that of Mrs. Ellen Cronin, fifty-six years old, and her daughter, Kate, twenty-six years old. They had died within twenty-four hours of each other. Mrs. Cronin succumbed to the heat on Monday and her daughter's death was due to grief. Mother and daughter had never been separated. The bodies were borne to Calvary Cemetery, where they were laid side by side.

—*New York Times*
July 5, 1901

Cigarettes May Have Caused Death

NEW YORK- Excessive smoking of cigarettes it is believed caused the death of

Hector Brown, seventeen years old, of 120 West One Hundred and Twenty-seventh Street, at 9 o'clock last evening. He was talking to his sweetheart, Mollie Diegan, of 426 St. Nicholas Avenue before her door when he suddenly placed his hand over his heart and said "I am very sick," and fell to the sidewalk. The girl screamed and Policeman John J. Dunn called an ambulance from the J. Hood Wright Hospital, but before it arrived the boy was dead. The body was taken to the West One Hundred and Twenty-fifth Street Police Station, where it was claimed by his mother.

—*New York Times*
November 8, 1901

In 1860, the population of the state was 3,880,735. Today over 19,306,183 people call the Empire State their home.

Killed In A Church
Sexton Of Church Of The Strangers Falls Down Stairs

NEW YORK- Gustav Buchia, forty years old, sexton of the Church of the Strangers, at Forty-seventh Street and Eighth Avenue, fell down a flight of steps in the church last night and was killed. He and his assistant Bernard Keenan had been cleaning the church after the regular Wednesday night services.

Buchia was sweeping at the top of a staircase in the rear of the church when he lost his balance and fell to the stone pavement below.

—New York Times
December 12, 1901

Excitement Was Fatal
Brooklyn Manufacturer Dropped Dead After Chasing Boys From His Home

BROOKLYN- Excitement caused the death yesterday of John Bartlett, a well-to-do retired saw manufacturer, at his home, 1085 Lafayette Avenue, Brooklyn. While sitting at an open front window yesterday morning he was annoyed by a crowd of boys in a near-by open lot who were continually throwing a ball against the side of his house. Mr. Bartlett, who was sixty-two years old, called to the boys to desist and finally determined to go out and drive them away.

While crossing his yard he failed to notice a wire screen fence, and he ran into it with such force that the fence collapsed, and he went down with it. Although uninjured he became greatly excited and on returning to his house he began to relate the annoyance of the boys to members of his family, when he suddenly fell over dead.

—New York Times
June 21, 1902

Fly Caused Blood Poisoning
Brooklyn Man, Who Had One Of His Thumbs Stung, Died In Great Agony.

BROOKLYN- George Lendhurst, a glass molder, who lived at 204 Ralph Street, Brooklyn, died in his home last night in extreme agony after having been stung on a thumb by a house fly two weeks ago. The swelling in the thumb extended to the arm, and from that to the body. A physician said it was a case of blood poisoning. The man's body swelled until it was twice its normal size. Lendhurst was a married man fifty-six years of age, and he had two children.

—New York Times
September 11, 1902

Brothers Die At Christmas
Richard Eaikens Found Stricken As Robert Was A Year Ago

NEW YORK- In two consecutive years Christmas Day has brought a strange death to members of the Eaikens family. Richard Eaikens, thirty-four years old, yesterday morning was found dying in the hallway of the house where he lives at 300 Third Avenue by Fred Eaton, another tenant. Policeman Hodgins of the East Twenty-second Street Station, summoned an ambulance with Dr. Hyde from Belleville Hospital, but the man died without speaking before it arrived.

Some think that he fell over the banisters, others that he died of apoplexy. There were no external evidences of injury. Eaikens was night watchman at the Continental Hotel, Broadway and Twentieth Street, and leaves a widow and two young daughters. On Christmas day of last year, Robert Eaikens, twenty-six years old, brother of the victim of yesterday's fatality, died under circumstances almost precisely similar at his home, 232 East Twenty-fourth Street.

—New York Times
December 26, 1902

He Hit A Man Too Hard
Cut On Hand From Antagonist's Teeth Caused Fatal Blood Poisoning

NEW YORK- Anton Anderson, fifty-two years old, of 18 Sector Street, died of blood poisoning in the Hudson Street Hospital yesterday because he hit a man too hard in the mouth Dec. 19 during a fight. Anderson punched his antagonist in the mouth with his right hand, the teeth of the other man cutting his fingers severely. Anderson's hand began to swell almost immediately and he went to the hospital for treatment. The surgeons there told him he would have to have the hand amputated but Anderson would not agree to let them do it. At last, when the swelling had spread to his arm, the man consented to let his hand be taken off. It was too late then and he died in agony.

—New York Times
December 26, 1902

Lost Life Over A Nickel
Elevated Road Passenger Killed After A Dispute With Chopper. Employee Says The Man Tried To Avoid Paying Fare. Jumped Or Was Thrown To Street, And Arrest Is Made.

NEW YORK- Although he had $2.47 in his pocket, a man lost his life yesterday afternoon because, it is asserted, he was unwilling to pay 5 cents for a ride on the elevated railroad. After an altercation with the ticket chopper on the down-town plat-

CHAPTER 1 BIZARRE DEATHS

form of the Third Avenue line's Fourteenth Street station, the man fell, or was pushed over the railing to the sidewalk. This was at 3:15 o'clock. Less than two hours later, a policeman having found him lying unconscious with a fractured skull, he died in Bellevue Hospital.

From the writing on a railway pass found in the victim's possession, it was assumed by the police that he was F. E. Bailey, forty years old, a levelman employed on the New Rochelle-Mount Vernon Division of the New York, New Haven and Hartford Railroad, but up to a late hour last night no one had appeared to verify the identification.

In the meantime Detective Kahn of the Fifth Street Police Station arrested John King, the ticket chopper on the station where the man is said to have tried to dodge his fare. King, who lives at 317 East Fifty-sixth Street, was charges with homicide, though he made a statement to the effect that the victim jumped from the platform voluntarily. Bailey, if that was his name, was seen to fall from the station by a crowd of pedestrians, who surrounded his prostrate form and attracted the attention of Policeman Junker. An ambulance was called, which carried the man to the hospital. Then Junker made his report to Sergt. McNaught, at the station, and the latter sent out Detective Kahn to investigate. The detective found that King, the ticket chopper, had left his post at Fourteenth Street, but from a description given by Junker he was located finally at the Thirty-fourth Street station.

King said he was standing beside his box when the stranger slipped into one of the exit gates and hence into the waiting room. He was informed of the man's presence by a passenger who had paid his fare. In a minute a train pulled in. The stranger left the waiting room and started to get aboard. King shouted for the ticket, but he got some talk instead. While they were argu-

ing the train left, and then, according to the chopper, the man pushed him from the platform to the tracks, so that he barely escaped hitting the third rail.

King immediately scrambled up. He saw the stranger trying to open a door in the waiting room, apparently thinking that was a way to leave the station. The chopper, according to his statement, ran down the north flight of stairs to find a policeman. Not finding one, he crossed Fourteenth Street, and began to ascend the south stairway. As he did so he saw the stranger jump from the station above, as though to get out of his (King's) way. Policeman Junker finally managed to get the names of three witnesses. They were Peter Harchom of 205 East Seventy-seventh Street, S. S. Brown of 82 Wall Street, and the Rev. John Alexander Gray of 212 East Twelfth Street.

Mr. Gray, when seen at his home last night, told a reporter that he was standing on the platform of the station waiting for a train when he saw King and the man who was afterward killed arguing about a ticket. The next thing Mr. Gray saw was King lying on the tracks. He said he saw King spring to his feet just in time to avoid an approaching train, jump to the platform, and dart down the steps to the street, while the man with whom he had been arguing rushed down on the other side. Mr. Gray said he did not see the man fall or jump from the platform.

—*New York Times*
September 25, 1903

Imagination
Caused This Man's Death

NEW YORK- That imagination alone can bring about death has been proven by the amazing case of Thomas Flynn, who has just died in St. Mary's Hospital, New York, from hydrophobia. It was conclusively proved at the autopsy that Flynn had never been bitten or even scratched by dog or other animal, and how he came to develop rabies puzzled the entire hospital staff until light was thrown on the mystery by a member of Flynn's family. Flynn's son asserted that his father was possessed of so vivid an imagination that he could make himself believe so absolutely in being the victim of a disease that after a few days the malady would actually make its appearance.

This explanation was laughed at by the medical men, and a thorough investigation of Flynn's antecedents was made. The result conclusively proved that not only had the unfortunate man never been bitten by any animal, but that neither was there any record of any member of his family ever having been bitten, and therefore the only possible chance of infection was negative. Flynn, it developed, was a hypnotist and took unnatural interest in hydrophobia cases, eagerly reading the numerous descriptive accounts of the terrible complaint in the daily papers. Over and over again he assured his friends that he should die of rabies, and at last he developed peculiar symptoms. When he attempted to swallow he had a convulsion. Dr. Daniel Juston was sent for, and after examining the patient he declared he was suffering from hydrophobia and ordered his removal to the hospital, where he died in great agony, barking and frothing at the mouth.

The only examination is that Flynn was a victim of auto-suggestion of self-hypnotism, a few cases of which are on record. Dr. Charles W. Brandenburgh, professor of therapeutic suggestion in the New York Electric College, declared that Flynn's case was the most extraordinary that had ever come under his notice, and he thinks that the man must certainly have put himself into a condition resembling hydrophobia by auto-suggestion.

It is not doubted by expert physicians that imagination can produce other diseases, such as consumption and heart disease. A young girl, Miss Bessie Toworth, who lived near Newark, N.J., recently became convinced that she should die of consumption. She was apparently robust and healthy, but after a time her mother took her to a doctor, who pronounced her perfectly sound. The girl was not convinced, however, and on her return home began to grow weak,, refused food, lost flesh and gradually sank into a decline. Her lungs became affected, and in less than six months she was dead, as a result, the doctors declared, simply of imagination.

—*Dallas Morning News*
December 13, 1903

Child's Death
Kills Mother
Mrs. Morse's Grief Brings On
Attack Of Heart Disease

BROOKLYN- Deep grief over the passing away of her young son, who died on Friday last, is said to have led to the death yesterday morning of Mrs. Lillian Morse, thirty-six years old, at her home, 40 ½ North Oxford Street, Brooklyn. The boy Frederick, five years old, died on Friday night as a result of injuries he received in a fall. After the funeral services in the house on Sunday night the mother became prostrated and late that night Dr. M. Amador of 187 Park Avenue was called in.

Dr. Amador says he found the woman in convulsions. She died soon after midnight. Dr. Emil F. Hartung, the Coroner's physician, has been directed to determine the cause of Mrs. Morse's death. The body of the boy has not yet been taken to the cemetery, and mother and son will be buried together this afternoon. It is believed that Mrs. Morse's death was due to an attack of heart disease brought on by hysterical grief.

—New York Times
May 3, 1904

Dies On Friend's Coffin
Woman Falls Dead
While Gazing On Features
Of Departed Companion

BROOKLYN- While gazing at the dead face of a lifelong woman friend, the coffin

lid having been reopened at her request. Mrs. Mary Reeves of Brooklyn has fallen dead across the casket. Mrs. Reeves had not the strength to take farewell of her dead friend when the other mourners did so, but as the pallbearers made ready to carry out the coffin she begged then to remove the cover. Looking upon the corpse she fell forward and expired from heart failure. The tragedy causes a postponement of the funeral.

—Dallas Morning News
September 23, 1904

The first American chess tournament was held in New York in 1843.

Died
On Her Sister's Grave
Remarkable Incident Which Caused
Death Of Young Jewish Girl In
Brooklyn Cemetery

BROOKLYN- Death came to a beautiful young Hebrew girl in Washington Cemetery, Brooklyn, in a manner probably unparalleled. Rising from the grave of her twin sister, where she had been praying, the heavy tombstone fell upon her, killing her instantly.

Three rabbis, to each of whom she had paid 50c to pray over the grave, were standing by her when the strange accident occurred. The prayers that were offered by the rabbis did not appease the young woman's grief, and when they had finished she fell sobbing and praying in the mound. Her prayer finished, she started to rise to her feet, and as she did so clutched at the tombstone for support. It crumbled at its base and she was caught beneath it. Her body lay pinioned under the stone until a tramp, who had been begging among those in the cemetery, ran to the spot and rolled the heavy weight from the lifeless form.

Two men, the builders of the monument, were arrested and locked in the Parkville police station as being responsible for her death by improperly setting the stone. The girl was identified some time after her death as Yetta Manhattan. Mr. Beyer, the girl's grandfather, told a pathetic story of her life. He said the twin sisters were attached to each other, and when Rosa Berkowitz died, two years ago, Yetta had nearly gone insane with grief. This summer, he said friends had taken her to the Catskill Mountains, but all the while she had continued to grieve for her sister. Often she had prayed that she might die and be buried by her sister Rosa's side, and now, he said, her prayer had been answered.

—*Dallas Morning News*
September 18, 1904

Born, Died And Buried On Same Day
Peculiar Coincidence In The Case Of Auburn Neighbors

AUBURN- Hugh D. Crawford and Mrs. John Dates, who were neighbors, died today about the same time. They were born on the same day, fifty-one years ago. The funeral of the former will be held at the house on Wednesday, and that of the latter at the Holy Family Church on the same day.

—*Syracuse Post Standard*
May 21, 1907

Singular Coincidence
Old Friends Die Within An Hour Of Each Other

OSWEGO- The death in Rochester yesterday morning at 10 o'clock of Richard J. Parkin, formerly of this city, and the finding of the dead body of "Chawd" Bryan in his boarding house here an hour or so later is regarded by many as a peculiar coincidence. As young men both were warm personal friends. They belonged to the same hose company in the old volunteer department, De Wolf hose No. 7, the organization of the town, and that both should die with an hour of each other is considered remarkable by their friends.

Mr. Parkin had been sick for two or three years, but Mr. Bryan had worked at the carpenter bench in the R. W. & O. Shops Friday, where he was employed. Both were good men; they had lived clean upright lives, and their deaths are regretted by wide circles of firmness. Mr. Parkin, since leaving Oswego ten years ago, has conducted the cigar stand at the Hotel Eggleston, Rochester.

—*Syracuse Herald*
January 5, 1908

Tragic Coincidence
Two Tea Merchants On The Same Street Commit Suicide

BROOKLYN- By a tragic coincidence two prosperous tea merchants in Brooklyn, doing business independently of each other on the same street, killed themselves yesterday. The first to end his life was Joseph M. Becker, 64 years old. He was found dead in bed with a gas tube in his mouth, at the Palace Hotel, where he had registered as "J. Bulger, New York."

Some time ago Becker moved from his old home and it was not until 10 P.M. that the police notified the family of the suicide. He left a widow, two daughters, both unmarried, and two sons. Worry over the recent panic was said to have unbalanced his mind.
Frederick W. Chapney, 46 years old, also in the tea business, shot himself to death in a saloon. According to Dr. Sharpe, the family physician, Chapney had been ailing with diabetes for some time. He leaves a widow.

—*Syracuse Herald*
November 28, 1908

Drops Dead
At Religious Meeting

NEW YORK- Peter Bellner, 75 years old, and old-time sailor, who recently had been living at the New York-Salvation Army Hotel in Chatham Square, fell dead last night as he was "testifying" at a religious meeting in the Salvation Army barracks at 94 Cherry Street.

—*New York Times*
January 4, 1909

A Strange Coincidence

MIDDLETOWN- The deaths of William H. O'Neal of Goshen, and Mrs. James M. Price of this city, being a rather strange coincidence to the family of Ora G. O'Neal of this city. The Messrs. O'Neal were cousins and Mrs. Price was the wife of Mrs. O'Neal's uncle. Their deaths occurred at about the same time and the funerals were held to-day at the same hour. Mr. O'Neal went to Goshen to attend the funeral of his cousin and Mrs. O'Neal attended the funeral of Mrs. Price.

—*Middletown Daily Times*
January 23, 1909

Dies At Funeral

OLEAN- While attending the funeral of Michael Downey at Mt. Morris Monday, John Dolan dropped dead at the grave and would have fallen in had he not been caught. He was 78 years old.

—*Olean Evening Times*
March 3, 1909

Girl's Strange Death
Suddenly Became Unconscious At Church Sunday And Died Yesterday

ROSE- Yesterday morning at the home of Alonzo Case in this village occurred the sudden death of Miss Dorothy Desmond, the 16-year-old daughter of Truman Desmond of East Rose. Miss Desmond had been in her normal health and attended a union service in the Methodist church at Rose last Sunday evening. She was not in her seat until the service was over. At the close of the service she walked out on the porch and fell down. She was picked up unconscious and carried to the home of Alonzo Case. Physicians were summoned and worked over her for many hours, but she never regained consciousness. Physicians were unable to determine the cause of her death. She is survived by her father. Her mother died many years ago.

—*The Syracuse Herald*
May 5, 1909

Dies From Parrot's Bite

ALBANY- A parrot's bite was responsible for the death of William Cluchy, 63 years old. On April 20th Cluchy, who is a builder, was playing with a pet parrot in his home in Sycamore Street. The parrot struck him with a severe blow, sinking its bill into the fleshy part of one finger, tearing the flesh loose from the bone. The parrot clung to the finger and it was necessary for Cluchy to nearly choke the bird to death before he could force it to release its hold. Cluchy thought little of the hurt at the time. He washed the wound and dressed it himself. The wound was infected, and in five days the finger was greatly swollen, and the swelling extended to the hand and was working up the arm slowly. Cluchy went to the Emergency hospital and was put to bed. He suffered pain continuously. He was delirious a part of the time. Then pneumonia set in and with the complications doctors were unable to save his life. He died on Thursday afternoon.

—*Syracuse Herald*
May 19, 1909

Strange Coincidence

MIDDLETOWN- Henry S. Pound, 70 years old, and Increase C. Jordon, 60, for many years composing the well-known firm of wholesale milk dealers, are dead at their home in this city. They were taken ill about the same time and died within six hours of each other. They were members of the New York Milk Exchange.

—*Dunkirk Evening Observer*
May 26, 1909

Prank Caused Death

MEDFORD- J. C. Tracy, a contractor of Medford L. I., last night refused to divulge the names of boys whose prank had resulted in the death of his son. "I am sure the boys acted only in sport," he said, "and I would not for the world make public their names and cause their families any of the grief we suffer."

George Tracy was 9 years old. He died yesterday afternoon at the Freeport L. I. Hospital. Mystery surrounded the death from the fact that the father had rushed him forty miles over the country for an operation. The lad's death is said to have been the result of his being tied to a tree by playmates. The ropes were bound so tight as to cause internal injures. "My son was playing, not with older boys," said the father "but with good friends about his own age.

They got a rope and tied him to a tree in the spirit of fun. They are manly little chaps and are as much grieved over the affair as we are. There is already trouble enough without adding that of publicity to the families of the boys whose innocent act caused my child's death."

—*Syracuse Herald*
July 14, 1909

Dies At His Mother's Grave
Franklin H. Baxter Falls Dead In St. Peter's Churchyard, Westchester.

WESTCHESTER- Franklin H. Baxter of 15 South Tenth Avenue, Mount Vernon, the last member of one of the earliest families to settle in the village of Westchester, dropped dead yesterday in St. Peter's churchyard, Westchester, as he left the graves of his father and mother. Baxter, who was 28 years old and unmarried, was accustomed to visit the churchyard daily, and had not missed a day, it was said, since the death of his father, three years ago. His mother died a year later.

Young Baxter had spent the better part of an hour in the churchyard, and stopped to speak to two gravediggers as he was leaving. Suddenly he uttered a cry and fell into a wheelbarrow which stood beside the open grave the men were digging. They summoned a doctor, but by the time he arrived Baxter was dead of heart disease.

—*New York Times*
July 17, 1909

Strange Fatalities

MIDDLETOWN- Mrs. Thomas Southwell, of this city, had the privilege of exhibiting bric-a-brac and souvenirs at the Sullivan County Fair next week. The fact of her having secured that privilege calls out a very peculiar and unexplainable fatality in the Southwell family. William Southwell, for several years the bric-a-brac and souvenir man at the Sullivan County Fair, died very suddenly four years ago. His wife rented the privilege and exhibited at the fair and the following year she died. Thomas Southwell, a brother of William, rented the fair privilege last year and shortly after the fair he died.

—*Middletown Daily Times Press*
August 14, 1909

Drops Dead
In A Jury Box

BROOKLYN- Henry Brunner, a Brooklyn merchant, dropped dead in the jury box to-day as he stood to answer to his name at the roll call. He answered "present," turned as if to sit down and fell into a heap on the floor.

—*Syracuse Post Standard*
February 22, 1910

Coincidence
Of Two Deaths

SYRACUSE- The coincidence of the two deaths followed even to the aliments of the mother and son. Both had caught a cold that ran into quick pneumonia and death within twelve hours of the attack.

—*Syracuse Post Standard*
April 2, 1910

Rice In Bride's Ear
Caused Her Death
After Ten Years Of Suffering

NEW YORK- A grain of rice which lodged in her ear the day of her wedding ten years ago is believed to have caused the death yesterday of Mrs. Ana Cummings at the Post Graduate Hospital. According to physicians, fruitless operations to remove the kernel of grain were performed several times during Mrs. Cummings' wedded life. The rice grain finally brought about inflammation of the brain.

—*Dunkirk Evening Observer*
May 3, 1910

Death's Strange
Coincidence

OLEAN- At 7 o'clock this morning Erwin, the 8-month-old son of Mr. and Mrs. August Sigel of 1203 Putnam Street died after a long illness of cholera infantum. The funeral announcement will be made later. Just a year ago to-day Mr. and Mrs. Sigel lost another child, Erwald, from the same disease and there was but a month's difference in the ages of the children at the time of their death.

—Olean Evening Times
September 13, 1910

EXTRA! EXTRA!

New York City has 722 miles of subway track.

Knee Fracture Caused Death

Philip Sharrer Was Not Victim Of Diabetes As Supposed. His Case An Unusual One. Autopsy Showed All Vital Organs In Normal Condition. Was Injured By Fall From Railroad Coach.

SYRACUSE- Exhaustion, following a fracture of the knee, it was learned yesterday, caused the death of Philip Sharrer of No. 401 Gifford Street, whose funeral is to be held this afternoon. Although he had

been under the care of a physician who was treating him for diabetes prior to the time he was accidentally thrown from the steps of a passenger coach on the New York Central two weeks ago at Buffalo, it was not until an autopsy had been performed that it was found the accident was directly the cause of his death.

After the accident Mr. Sharrer was brought home and was under the care of Dr. W. L. Hartman, surgeon for the railroad company. The doctor called on him Tuesday morning and he was apparently doing well. An hour later he died suddenly in his chair. Friends thought it was his old trouble that had caused his death.

Vital Organs Nearly Normal

An autopsy was performed Wednesday under Dr. Hartman's supervision. All the vital organs were found to be in practically normal condition, and although it was found Mr. Sharrer had other trouble, it was Dr. Hartman's conclusion that the injury to his knee caused death. The death certificate signed by Dr. Hartman yesterday gives as the cause of death "fracture of the knee joint from being thrown from train," and the contributory cause "exhaustion." When asked if the case was not an unusual one, Dr, Hartman said: "Such cases arise occasionally and we cannot account for them. While the man had some other troubles there was nothing serious enough to have caused his death."

—The Syracuse Post Standard
December 16, 1910

Bound To Die Stays In Bed Until He Does

**Coroner Will Investigate Strange Case Of Jerome Hackett.
He Did Not Want To Live.
Aged Cicero Farmer, After Recovering From Accident, Would Not Get Up And Sometimes Refused To Eat.**

CICERO- When Coroner George R. Kinne begins to-day an investigation of the death of Jerome Hackett, which occurred at 6 o'clock yesterday morning at the latter's home, one mile east of Cicero, he will take up one of the most unusual cases that has come to the attention of an Onondaga County coroner in years.

After having recovered from injuries received three years ago, when he was struck by an automobile, Mr. Hackett took to his bed and declared that he didn't want to get well. There were times when he would refuse to eat and although he never attempted to end his life, he refused to leave his bed, and, according to his physician, this resulted in gradually weakening him until he died.

After a talk yesterday with Dr. A. G. Tripp of Cicero, who had previously attended Mr. Hackett, Coroner Kline said the man had probably died of arterial sclerosis, a hardening of the tissues of the arteries. Mr. Hackett, who was 72 years old, was for many years a well known and prosperous farmer in the town of Cicero. His house stands on the Bridgeport road near where the tracks of the Syracuse & South Bay trolley line leave that highway.

Three years ago, last June, Mr. Hackett was struck by an automobile near his home. His collar bone was broken and he was hurt internally. For some time Mr. Hackett was under the care of Dr. Tripp, the family physician. There were no symptoms of any head injury and Hackett, to all appearances had apparently recovered fully and was able to get up when his mental condition seemed to weaken. It was then that the man declared he did not want to get well and refused to leave his bed, although there was apparently no reason for it other than an unsound mind.

Because of lack of exercise and his refusal at times to eat, Mr. Hackett's condition weakened all the time he was in bed. He was not under the care of a physician and refused to have the services of one. Dr. Tripp, when called to attend other members of the family when they were ill, saw Mr. Hackett, but not professionally. Dr. Tripp was called to attend him December 9, but not since then. Mr. Hackett is survived by his wife, by one son, Charles Hackett, and by three daughters, Mrs. Clinton Weaver of Bridgeport, Mrs. Charles Fisher of Cicero and Miss Emma Hackett, living at home.

—*Syracuse Post Standard*
December 27, 1910

Sisters, Reunited Here After Long Separation
Pass Away In 2 Days.
Daughter Returning From Mrs. Stevens' Funeral Hears Of Aunt's Death.

SYRACUSE- Mrs. Henrietta Shaver died last night, forty-eight hours after the death of her only sister, Mrs. Lydia Stevens, whose funeral was held yesterday afternoon. After having been separated for a number of years, Mrs. Shaver came from Chicago to Syracuse about one year ago to live with her sister and the latter's daughter, Miss Maud Stevens, at No. 319 Merriman Avenue.

Last summer, Mrs. Shaver became ill, and upon the advice of a Manlius physician she was sent to the Elmhurst Sanitarium, No. 630 Park Avenue, where her death occurred last night. She was 74 years old, four years older than Mrs. Stevens. The death of the latter occurred Friday night at her home on Merriman Avenue. Mrs. Stevens called upon Mrs. Shaver a number of times at the sanitarium until she, too, became ill and sickness again separated the two only to reunite them in death again yesterday. Prayer was said for Mrs. Stevens at No. 313 Merriman Avenue at noon yesterday, after which A. C. Schumacher, undertaker, sent the body to Lacona for a funeral service and interment.

Her daughter, Miss Maud Stevens, had just returned home last evening when she learned that her aunt was dead. The latter's body will be taken to A. C. Schumacher's undertaking rooms to-day, and as soon as the necessary arrangements can be made will be taken to Chicago for interment. Mrs. Shaver had been a resident of Chicago for a number of years. Her husband died in that city and her body is to be placed beside that of her husband. Mrs. Stevens was the widow of William Jay Stevens of Lacona.

—*Syracuse Post Standard*
December 27, 1910

Ghosts

A Ghost In The Woods

**Two Hunters Mystified
In A Pike County Forest.
A Ghostly Apparition Peering At
Them From The Window Of A
Deserted Cabin.
Unable To Discover Any One Of
The Premises.
A Hut With A History.**

PORT JERVIS- Situated upon the edge of a dark swamp, in an isolated wilderness, near the Walker Pond, in Shohola Township, this county, has stood for many years a small, one-story log cabin. Just about dusk a few evenings ago, two Orange County hunters, passing within sight of the cabin, discovered a strange object peering at them from one of the windows. As they were some distance off they took it to be a man attired in his night garments.

Their curiosity was excited to know who occupied so lonely and dilapidated abut. They proceeded to go toward the cabin, and as they were walking their eyes rested steadily upon the strange object which appeared stationary. When they had neared to within a few yards of the cabin, the being, like a sudden flash, disappeared. The hunters halted for a moment, but finally resolved to approach the window. The panes of glass were found to be broken. They peered in but saw no one or any articles of furniture. They entered, made an examination of the premises, but their search revealed nothing, except now and then faint noises, as if made by some one in distress.

They were at once possessed with strange and unpleasant fancies. It was fast growing dark, and the stars were beginning to dimly twinkle, and they concluded to proceed on their way homeward. Having reached the edge of the swamp, they again glanced back at the cabin. To their utter surprise and astonishment, they saw a strange figure, standing in precisely the same attitude as before, peering at them. The hunters began to think some one was endeavoring to play a joke upon them, and they resolved to make it lively for the joker. They advanced to within throwing distance and commenced firing missiles.

They struck all about the window, and now and then one seemed to hit the mark at which it was directed, but not withstanding the object remained perfectly stationary. Determined to ferret out the mystery, they again advanced toward the cabin, but, as before, when they had neared to within the same distance, the vision again vanished. They finally concluded that the place was possessed with ghosts, hob-goblins, or something of the kind, and throwing their guns over their shoulders departed.

The cabin has a history. It has had numerous tenants, the last one living within its desolated walls being a person giving the name of Berger, who occupied it about eight or ten years ago, and claimed to have once been a successful merchant tailor in Norway. To all appearances he was a man apparently thirty-five years of age; but from his peculiar characteristics and feminine appearance, the stranger was believed to be a woman in disguise. Berger was well educated, spoke fair English, and was well versed upon almost any topic. His looks plainly denoted that he never done hard, muscular labor.

The property upon which the cabin stands is surrounded by a few acres of tillable land. In order to work it Berger bought a yoke of oxen, which, during his stay of about two years, were his sole companions. He had not even a dog or cat and he lived in a hermit-like manner. He was averse to receiving visitors, and when hunters were passing near his abode and he heard them, he would bar the doors and secrete himself until they were out of sight. His strange mode of living soon aroused the curiosity of the neighborhood, and often at night parties would approach to within seeing and hearing distance of the cabin, to ascertain, if possible, what the occupant busied himself at. Usually he would be heard singing church melodies and at times engaged in low conversation with himself.

He used neither lamp or candle, his only light being from the stove. On one occasion at night, two young men resolved to visit him. They walked cautiously to the door of the cabin and knocked. But the customary "walk in" was not heard. They knocked a second time, and louder, and still there came no response. They then walked around to a side window, where by the dim flickering light which came from within, they saw the occupant. He evidently had heard them for he was endeavoring to secrete himself. The visitors remained for some time, vainly waiting for admission when they returned home.

Their visit and strange reception soon became the all absorbing topic of conversation. There were many versions as to why Berger lived so strangely. Some believed him guilty of a great crime, after committing which he secreted himself in this isolated region in order to escape arrest. Others thought him a rich miner, with gold secreted about his premises. Be his strange mode of life attributed to whatever cause it may, Berger finally observed that he was exciting the suspicions of the neighborhood, and suddenly left for parts unknown. The cabin still stands, and had ever since been tenantless.

—*Port Jervis Evening Gazette*
February 16, 1878

A Coughing Ghost
Hair-raising Story Of A Haunted House At Little Falls

LITTLE FALLS- The latest sensation here is a haunted house. No. 29 Portens Street is a dwelling occupied by two families, that of James Carney on the first floor, and Mrs. Moynahan, a widow, and her children on the second. These families have occupied the house for the past two months. Of late they have been startled by ghostly and unusual noises, such as a dry, sepulchral cough and the slamming and opening of doors. If a door was closed it would suddenly spring open without the aid of visible hands, and if it was opened it would close with a slam in the same mysterious way.

In one of the rooms occupied by the Carneys after dark the dry coughing commences, so ghostlike in sound that as Mr. Carney describes it, it makes the hair rise on his head and can be distinctly heard all night long, and apparently comes from under the bed. Doors locked at night are found unlocked in the morning, and yet there are no signs that a human hand has unfastened them. The families being unable to solve the mystery of these ghostly manifestations have vacated the house. Last Monday night, the coughing and opening and closing of doors so demoralized them that they took refuge in one room. There were seven in all, but still the ghost was not disturbed by their presence, for it kept on coughing and making peculiar noises the entire night, and the coughing always proceeded from the same spot under the bed. It was a long and fearful night and the inmates of the haunted house clung to each other and waited with beating hearts and terror in their souls for the break of day, when the invisible spirit would vanish and the coughing cease. The night was one long to be remembered and they shiver now when they think of it. The following day after their unusual experience the premises were vacated.

—*Syracuse Herald*
April 15, 1888

Ghost Hurls Missiles
Oswego Custom House Janitor
Talks Of Giving Up His Fat Job

OSWEGO- The Democratic employees in the Custom House are greatly pleased that the civil service rules will retain them in office for an indefinite period, and that Collector Cooper will have to find good cause for their removal. There are several snug berths included in this list, some of which are of great importance, and carry good-sized salaries, which the Republicans would like to secure. The positions which are guarded include the janitors of the building, and already there is a contest on as to who shall have these berths, as there are rumors current that the present incumbents will be removed for cause.

But there is one janitor, "Charley" Smith, who says that he will not avail himself of the protection that the law gives him, as he thinks that his life is in danger. He firmly believes that the building is haunted and that some one is trying to do him bodily injury. "Charley" claims that he has seen the ghost and no amount of arguing on the part of his friends will convince him otherwise, at least not until they get ahold of the ghost and give him a thrashing.

The ghost frequents the upper story, and roams about the court room, where the civil service examinations are held. Smith says concerning his experience, "Why I saw one face to face, by jiminy gracious, and there is no doubt about it. This ghost threw twelve blocks of wood at me, and it has also hurled gas pipes and all sorts of other things. I am afraid of my life to go up there. You ask 'Doc' Mackin. He will tell you that it is no fake. Other fellows in the building will also tell you the same thing, and if the ghost doesn't quit bothering me I may give up the job."

—*Syracuse Sunday Herald*
January 30, 1898

Made Insane By Ghosts

TRENTON- Two inmates of the Trenton Jail were made insane by ghostly visitors. The jailers ridiculed them, but they insisted on their ghost story and finally were driven insane.

—*Dallas Morning News*
October 17, 1898

Taylor's Ghost
Seen Last Week By Belated Merrymakers.
The Terrible "Face Against The Pane" On The Somerville Pike.
Revealed By The Fitful Flashes Of Lightning On July Nights.
The Terror Of A Dancing Party Who Saw The Grinning Apparition.
Recalls The Story Of The Tragedy Enacted In The Old Stone House.
Mrs. Taylor Shot By Her Husband, Who Fled, But Returned And Hanged Himself At The Window.

SOMERVILLE- "The face against the pane," whose distorted features glance, it is said, from the rickety gable window of the old "Jack" Taylor house in the Somerville turnpike when the heat lightning glows on sultry summer nights and the thunder mutters among the Rossie bills, was seen again just before the dawn of Wednesday last by a party of country lads and lassies who had danced the night away at Kinney ball. It is only on a certain night in the latter part of July, and by the fitful blaze of lightning flashes alone, according to the tales told around the grocery stores of Wexatchie and Somerville, that the likeness of "Jack" Taylor, the murderer and suicide, can be seen grinning from the glass which mirrored his dead face as being hung swaying by a rope in the kitchen of his farmhouse, and the recent experience which the revelers of that neighborhood relate is in keeping with the old legend of the haunted house on the Somerville Pike.

The party of dancers returning last Wednesday morning from Kinney ball, where in the good old days stately Col. Hoyie Benton led the minuet with beauties of the once wealthy and aristocratic Sterling family, and whose floors have echoed to the dancing feet of five generations, included "Tommy" Carr, Brayton Turnbull and John Henry Beanheld, with a trio of young women of that neighborhood, whom they were escorting home. All were afoot and the party on approaching the lonely hollow in which the odd (Rest of article illegible)

—*Syracuse Herald*
July 30, 1889

Woodside's Haunted Well
**Woman And Children Chased By A
White-robed Figure.
Even Young Men
Scared Half Out Of Their Wits.
The Village People Have
Determined That The Cause Of
Terror Must Be Captured
Or Driven Away.
The Well Surrounded
By Armed Citizens.
Not A Good Place For A Practical
Joker To Be Caught.**

WOODSIDE- An old and moss-grown well, the source of the water supply of the people of Woodside Heights, was guarded to-night by armed and angry citizens, determined to solve a mystery. For days a white-robed figure has haunted the well, causing terror among the woman and children, and even putting young men to ignominious flight.

Because of a long drought, the residents of the heights have had to get their water from this well, which is in a shady nook reached by well-trodden paths winding to all oaths of the village. Most of the water carrying is done by the children.

Three days ago little Josie Winnie and George Caton went to the well with pitchers and palls. It was broad daylight. They were standing about the well when they heard a noise behind them, and, looking, saw hopping toward them, on all-fours what appeared to be a man wrapped in a white sheet. They screamed, dropped their palls and pitchers, and for a second were too frightened to stir. Then they fled.

Soon after this, Annie Robinson, fourteen years old, went to the well and the same figure rose before her, waved its arms, and silently glared at her. She says the white sheet evidently concealed a man of great

size, and powerful. She believed he is an escaped lunatic. He uttered no sound, but simply stood, and looked at her fiercely, with eyes that shone like flame.

Annie did not think the man was a practical joker. The thought that he was a (can't read) added to her speed in getting to her home in Cleveland Avenue. In rapid succession the children of J. Englefinger, Frank Caseman, and John Dietrich were sent home terrified and screaming by the apparition. Two young men, Charles Christensen and Thomas Robinson, had the strangest meeting of all with the "ghost of the well," each saw the sheeted figure. They were chased by it nearly a mile.

Robinson, who is eighteen years old and drives a wagon for August Burgess of Wood haven, was driving home early last evening. When he reached the old well he stopped and went to get some water to take to his home, about a mile away. He had scarcely reached the well, and had not even the time to send the bucket down, when he heard a heavy tread in the underbrush, and in a second a huge white figure stood before them. As he gazed the figure came rapidly toward him, with eyes ablaze and evidently bent on them.

Robinson, shaking with fear, made a wild dash for his wagon, lashed the horse into a mad gallop, and was off for home. Behind him, and as it appeared to him, coming on the wings of the wind, was the terrible white-sheeted demon. He reached his home in safety. His pursuer had given up the chase, and was nowhere in sight.

Christensen had to work harder to escape,

for he was on feet, and the white apparition proved to be a splendid sprinter. His experience came only an hour later than that of Robinson, and yet the man in white was not a bit fatigued, and Christensen declares he could almost feel the hot breath of his pursuer on the back of his neck as the two raced along.

In his flight the young man roused Mr. Englefinger's dogs, and their master came to the door to see what the trouble was. Christensen saw a haven of safety, and, putting all his waning strength into one last spurt, he plunged into Mr. Englefinger's arms, much to that gentleman's surprise. The ghost-laying party to-night consists of young Christensen's father, John Caton, J. Englefinger, John Dietrich, and Frank Caseman. There are as many opinions about the white figure as there are men in the party, but there is among them a grim determination to capture the object of terror.

Last night a few men went out on a search. They did not see the mysterious man, but found in the woods near the well a place where a human body had lain.

—*New York Times*
July 28, 1891

EXTRA! EXTRA!

The oldest cattle ranch in the U.S. was created way back in 1747 at Montauk.

An Ancestral Ghost
It Was A New York Apparition
And Its Habitat
The Van Cortlandt Manor House.
New York Woman Saw It.
It Was The Old Housekeeper
Of The Manor,
Unable To Rest Because Of
An Uneasy Conscience.
She Had Taken Family Silver.

NEW YORK- It is a real ghost story, and the beauty of it is that it is told by the woman who saw the ghost. It was some time ago that it happened, but it made such a distinct impression upon her mind that it is all as vivid as if it had happened but yesterday. She was not a professional hostess of ghosts, and at the time she received the mysterious visitation she was a pretty, healthy young girl, much more interested in getting a cool long night's rest than in all the mysterious things in the world. But she recognized her ghost when she saw it,

and she believes in it just as certainly now that she is a handsome matron with a daughter of her own as she did at the time of the occurrence.

It was a ghost worth seeing, too, for it was a real ancestral ghost, such as seldom seen in young America, and its midnight wanderers had caused stronger and older people than this young girl some very unpleasant moments; but until her experience it had never been visible. She was a Southern girl, and did not know the habitat of the ghost or the tradition of the family, though it was her own. All of which goes to prove that it was a bona fide ghost. No one would doubt it who heard the story from the lips of the woman who tells it—a woman well known in New York society as a clever member of a distinguished family. The house in which the ghost appeared is one in which all New Yorkers are acquainted—the old Van Cortlandt manor house. The young girl, however, was a stranger there, and it was her first night in the place.

To make the narrative interesting it is necessary to tell something of the history of the heroine. Her father, a man bearing a historical old Dutch name, had gone South on some business for the government a number of years before, fallen in love with a charming young Southern girl, and settled in Washington to live. There had been some property differences causing a little estrangement, as is often the case in well-conducted families. There was a good deal of strong feeling, and the Washington man had for a long time held no intercourse with the New York branch of the family. But after a time the father died, and the mother was glad to have her children know their father's people. A reconciliation took place, and in time the young daughter came on to make a visit.

She was stopping with an uncle and aunt, when one day came another uncle and aunt from the manor house in state and an old family coach to make a formal call upon this visiting relative, who was a stranger to them all, and also to take her away, if they could, to visit them. They had a house full of young people and she was sent to have the best kind of time a young girl could want.

So the little lady from Washington, quite a pretentious figure with her gown set out by the leg hoopskirt which was worn at that time, returned in the big coach with her hospitable relatives. The Van Cortlandt manor house is a large, rambling building, and at this time it was very well filled with guests, and there was only one large sleeping room vacant. This was on the ground floor, in one of the wings and quite away from the other sleeping rooms and was reached through a big summer parlor. There was also a large empty room, which the children used as a playroom, on the other side. The young guest must either occupy this room or share a room with some one else, and she immediately chose the former. (Unable to read the rest of story.)

—*New York Times*
October 16, 1898

The Van Cortlandt Manor House still stands today, providing history and tours.

Mystery Of Cherry Hill
**Haunted Flat Made Uninhabitable For Nineteen Years.
Ghost-scorning Tenants Assaulted And Their Furniture Thrown About By Invisible Visitors.**

NEW YORK- Within a stone's throw of the headquarters of the Square-Back Rangers, in Cherry Street, is a three room front flat, which had come near enough to being haunted, so that no tenant had remained more than a few hours within its walls for the goodly space of nineteen years. Tenants have presumed to move in only to hustle out after finding their furniture turned upside down and their handsome framed chromes turned to the wall by occult influences.

The bravest "guy" on Cherry Hill five years ago ventured to go into the hallway several hours after twilight. He could see nothing there, but he got a thump in the eye and also managed to get a swollen cheek. He said it was the nastiest scrap he ever ran up against.

An old French woman, nineteen years ago became agonized with grief over the loss of her husband, who had sickened and died in that flat. One night she took a blanket and a stout clothes line, and with their help hanged herself on the bedroom door. She was found dead in the morning and her body was taken down by the neighbors. Since that tragedy the flat has been uninhabitable. Cherry Hill lights hesitate to say that it is haunted because they do not believe that the ghost of the unfortunate French woman ever comes back to the scene of death. But, everybody in the old Fourth ward knows that there is something the matter with that flat.

There were the Ryans, who were just as respectable a family as ever lived on the hill, and they had no skeletons in their family closet to excite the sinister ill-will of the ghost. They moved into the flat— husband and wife and three children. About an hour after they had all gone to bed there was one of the greatest rackets that ever took place in a genuinely haunted house. The family woke up to see their furniture being thrown all over the flat by some invisible agency. The husband was punched in the face and the wife had her left eye blackened and the children came down with the whopping cough. All this happened in about ten minutes time. Six hours had been used to move into the flat, but it took that family just fifty minutes to get out with all their belongings.

Four or five other families tried their luck,

but the hoodoo was too alert and strong. Old Mike Finnegan could not stand it when his stove, which had been securely set up in position, dropped over on its side. Every kind of tenant had tried it except the Italians, and front flats on the hill are not accessible to them.

Nobody has ever seen anything in that flat which could cause a rumpus. Not a ghost had ever been detected. The flat is known on the hill as the "stable alley" and any spirit investigator who really wants to see the place can find it by asking the first longshoreman he meets walking on the hill for directions to the house where "Jackie" Haggerty lost the last shred of his reputation by letting himself get a black eye from the evil influence in the hallway. "Jackie" used to cut a good deal of ice in the social firmament of Cherry Hill before he queered himself in the haunted flat.

Psychical students can get more real information in five minutes spent in that flat after dark about the spirit business that they get now in a whole series of Winter lectures at a lyceum on the way brain molecules have of wagging on St. Patrick's eve and other great spirit occasions of the year. There is a man on the hill who had never been out to the Fourth Ward. He was born in the haunted flat before the evil days came upon the habitation, but he had not crossed the threshold of his birthplace for twenty years and all the profits of the Gambling Commission could not induce him to visit the scenes of his childhood. He says, though, that he does not believe the flat is haunted.

—*New York Times*
March 25, 1900

Say They Saw An Apparition

Five Young Women Declare That They Saw The Spirit Of A Dead Friend

YONKERS- Five young women of this city are certain they saw an apparition this morning. They claim they saw an exact picture of a dead friend, whose body lay on a bed in the room where they were, suddenly appear outlined against the wall surrounded by a cloud. The picture passed across the wall, and starting from one corner of the room passed in the opposite one and then dissolved.

The young women who claim to have seen this sight are Messes Rose Kearns, Rose McGowan, Minnie McGowan, Katie Kane, and Norah Smith. The young women who died was Julia R. Murray. She was eighteen years of age. She live with her family at 154 Ashburton Avenue. Two weeks ago she was taken ill with meningitis. Her death took place on Saturday. She was a devoted Christian and constant attendant at St. Joseph's Roman Catholic Church which is directly opposite the home of the girl.

The alleged apparition occurred about 4 o'clock this morning. In the room itself at the time were Miss Kearns, Miss Kane and the Misses McGowan. Miss Smith was sitting in the parlor so she could see into the room where the body lay. Miss Smith had been in the parlor, but had risen from her seat, crossed the parlor, and was about to step into the rear room when the apparition appeared. She dropped to the floor in a faint from which she was not revived for some time, and after the others had told the story as they saw it. The story they tell is this:

In the southwest corner of the room a cloud appeared. From it as it extended itself upward, appeared the form of a woman. The hands were crossed over the breast so that the palms rested near the shoulder. The head was thrown upward and somewhat backward. There was a crown of flowers on the head. The robe was a loose flowing one of white. On one point each of the five who say they saw this are very positive, and that is that the features were those of their dead friend as they knew her in life.

The apparition lasted but a second or two. It passed along the wall to the other corner. As it passed, the hands moved and the fingers were clasped in front of the breast as if in prayer. The cry of Miss Smith brought others to the room, but too late to see the apparition. The young women who did not faint were almost as helpless as if they had, but they soon revived and narrated what they claim to have seen. The funeral for the dead girl took place this morning as scheduled.

—*New York Times*
March 27, 1901

Cazenovia Is Haunted

**Strange Apparition Seen On The Streets At Night.
Great Excitement Prevails.
The Ghost Is Described As Wearing A Long White Flowing Robe And A White Hood Running Up To A Point—Has Its Favorite Haunts—Many Theories Have Been Proposed To Account For The Appearance Of The Strange Vision.**

CAZENOVIA- The usual clam of this quiet village has given way to unwanted excitement. Strong men do not venture out at night unarmed, and even the most daring urchins have suddenly discovered a new charm in staying at home. The cause of this state of things is the advent of some apparently unearthly object which wanders at will about the streets frightening men, women, and children.

The apparition is variously described as ranging in height from five to six feet. By some it is said to have a slight figure, while others, who claim to have good reason to know of what they are talking, desire it to be of much greater dimensions. It sulks behind hedges, in the shadow of buildings and glides between the lofty elms for which Cazenovia is noted. Its head is described as enclosed in a white hood which terminates in a point which always looks backward and forward as the ghost glides over the ground. The figure below the head is robed in a long flowing mantle of snowy whiteness.

Several times on its nightly errands it has been seen to display threatening a long, rusty knife and a revolver which glistens in the moonlight. Its favorite haunts seem to be about the old skating rink, the Lehigh Valley Station, and Sullivan Street. A few nights ago several boys were chased into a house by the strange object, but the same night it also was pursued through a vacant lot by three men, when it suddenly disappeared.

Various Deeds Undone

One evening some such factory hands were walking their way homeward along the railroad tracks boasting the heroic deeds they would do if the "fake" apparition should appear to them, when on rounding a curve they were surprised by the subject of their conversation. Without a moment's hesitation they took to their heels and did not stop for breath until they burst excitedly into their own homes. Some insist that it is simply some boy out for a little fun. Others say it is merely a delusion. Still others believe it to be a sick man slightly demented. Another theory is that it is some one having the interest of the village at heart and it is trying to do the young lads a service by frightening them off the streets at night.

—*Syracuse Post Standard*
December 8, 1901

Chittenango is the home of author L. Frank Baum, who wrote *Wizard of Oz*.

Joseph Jefferson, Walt Whitman, Robert Bonner and other noted men. Mr. Jackson's wife died last July. They were married twenty-seven years ago Saturday and in commemoration of the anniversary Mr. Jackson invited man guests, to each of whom he gave a printed souvenir. He told the guest that ever since his wife's death she had been by his side day and night in the spirit. He talked with her, and she often sang to him. He had also received letters from her. He said he expected to receive a communication from her on their wedding anniversary.

—*Milwaukee Journal*
January 13, 1903

Baldwinsville's Haunted House

BALDWINSVILLE- The neighbors in a certain part of Baldwinsville believe that a house at which a woman met a violent death is haunted by her spirit. The Sunday Herald gives pictures and relates the stories of the believers in the supernatural.

—*Syracuse Evening Herald*
December 11, 1903

"Ghost" In Charge Of Police

SYRACUSE- The Otisco Street "ghost" is now installed at Police Headquarters. It was taken there by a policeman, who notified the owner that Captain Quigley desired an interview with her at the police station yesterday morning at 9 o'clock. The captain was prepared to give the woman some advice about scaring people, but she did not appear.

—*Syracuse Post Standard*
September 21, 1902

Celebrates Anniversary With Dead Wife's Spirit

BROOKLYN- A strange wedding anniversary was celebrated in Brooklyn by Joseph Jackson, the intimate friend of

Sounds Of
Death Struggle
Heard in Haunted House
A Cortland Tenement,
Once Occupied By Italian Laborers,
Shunned By Young And Old.
Unearthly Noises Said To Have
Been Heard.

CORTLAND- Over in the eastern portion of the city, on one of the leading streets, stands a solidly built house that can be purchased for less than half its value. It is a veritable "white elephant" upon the owner's hands.

Several months ago it sheltered a gang of Italian laborers, but now it is impossible to secure tenants, and the house stands singularly apart from its neighbors, forlorn and lonely, the wintry winds rattling the loosened shutters or scurrying through the broken window panes.

Years ago this house was one of the best upon the street. Now it is shunned by all. Small boys going home at night cross to the other side, and with many a furtive glance scamper homeward. Some of the older people even glance askance as they pass the place. Two years ago, it is said, while a gang of Italians occupied the place, one of their number suddenly came up missing. A few weeks went by and then strange noises began to be heard. Unearthly moans, the noise of a scuffle and a fall and the dripping of blood are also said to have been heard many times.

The windows rattle whether a wind blows or not. The Italians hastily decamped, and since then the house had been regarded as haunted. Members of the police force aver that they have seen strange lights flashing from window to window.

—Syracuse Post Standard
March 17, 1906

Saw Her Uncle's Face
Terranova Girl Complained To
Witness Of Being Haunted.
Mrs. Vasta Testifies That The
Defendant Also Declared That She
Heard Her Victim Cry To Her.
Experts Called To Testify As To Her
Mental Condition.

NEW YORK- Mrs. Adele Vasta, the first witness in the trial of Josephine Terranova on a charge of murdering her aunt, Mrs. Concetta Reggio, testified to-day that when she visited the accused girl in a cell in the Tombs prison last February the girl told her that she had seen the face of her uncle, whom she killed, on the wall of her cell. Mrs. Vasta is a parish visitor of the Catholic church who visited Mrs. Terranova to give her religious consolation. She testified:.....................

"I saw that the girl had her apron hanging on the wall of her cell. When I asked her about it she said her uncle's spirit had appeared to her in the night and she put the apron over the spot to hide him from her sight. She stared at me and cried out while I was there, 'There he is now.' She also said she heard her uncle's cry to her. I was so frightened and upset that I couldn't go back again for a week."

The girl, she said had complained of pains and ringing noises in her head. After this witness had been excused the defense began calling experts to testify as to Josephine's sanity. Dr. Henry Tyson, an oculist of the College of Physicians and Surgeons, said that the girl had an affection of the eyes which is associated either with cases of mental disorder or of hysteria.

—*Syracuse Herald*
May 23, 1906

Marsh "Spook House" Sold

MIDDLETOWN- The famous "spook house" on Benton Avenue, this city, formerly occupied by Luther M. Marsh, the noted lawyer, has been sold to Dr. H. R. Kline of Philadelphia. He will turn the mansion into a sanitarium. Several weeks ago an effort was made to sell the property at public auction, but no bidders appeared. Superstitious people asserted that the house was haunted.

The property belonged to the estate of Clarissa J. Huyler, the alleged medium, who for years duped Marsh. It was here that Mrs. Huyler elicited the greater part of one of Marsh's well known hooks, "The Voice From the Patriarches."

—*Syracuse Herald*
July 26, 1906

This Oswego Girl Very Badly Scared
Ran Screaming Down East Second Street, Declaring She Had Seen An Apparition Near The Storehouse Of Ames Iron Works.

OSWEGO- Early this evening a young woman whose name could not be learned ran screaming down the railroad tracks in East Second Street, near the Ames Iron Works. Two boys who were proceeding along East Seneca Street ran to her assistance.

She was returning, she said to her home in the Second Ward and she had occasion to pass along East Cayuga Street between Second and Third, and just as she arrived at a point opposite the storehouse used by the Ames Company she was startled by seeing a white object that seemed to rise directly from the ground extend it arms towards her in an entreating manner, and all the time emitting a sort of rumbling noise, such as would be made by sliding coal through an iron slide, only it was not so distinct.

The object, according to the girl, seemed to be suspended between the sky and the earth, with no visible means of support either from above or below, and all the time waved from side to side in a fantastic manner. The young woman was stunned at first from the shock but finally recovered the use of her extremities and ran from the spot with all possible speed. According to the boys she seemed to be in a most excited condition and talked about ghosts and white things that had come to haunt her. She recovered in a short time and departed on her way home.

Some credence might be placed in the story by those who believe in the supernatural from the fact that about a month ago while workman were engaged in that vicinity in excavating for the purpose of laying a walk from the street to the Ames storehouse a skeleton was discovered with only about a foot of earth. Coroner C. J. Vowinkle was notified on that occasion and visited the scene and pronounced the find to be the skeleton of a woman who, according to surrounding, had been in the ground almost a century.

Local historians remembered a legend that had come to them form their grandfathers to the effect that along the area when the Indians were camped in the parts and shared the game in the surrounding woods with their white brethren the tents of the braves were pitched at this very place. It was supposed that the skeleton was the

remains of a squaw who met her death there.

—*Syracuse Post Standard*
October 20, 1906

You can find the remains of the Ames Iron Works at the Railroad Museum in Oswego.

Badly Frightened Youth

OTISVILLE- While passing the cemetery, adjoining Holy Name Church, one of our village youths was badly frightened by an apparition, rising from a newly made grave. He now acknowledges he is a firm believer in ghosts.

—*Middletown*
Orange County Times Press
May 8, 1908

Ghosts In Studio

**Stuart Travis, The Artist, Haunted
By Guests From Beyond.
They Snore And Lock Doors.
Dog Was Frightened By Strange
Sounds And Model Found Herself
Unable To Open A Door.
Mysterious Voices Too.**

NEW YORK- Stuart Travis, the artist, known among his brother artists as the painter of pretty women and smart men, has been entertaining his friends lately with stories of queer doings in and about his studio, on the second floor of the old studio building, at No. 112 West Fortieth Street, New York. Mr. Travis himself has nothing whatever to do with these events, but he would like very much to know who has. That they happen he is convinced. He cites Buttons, his pet bull terrier, as a witness to the truth of everything he says about the mystery that is now the talk of certain members of New York's artistic colony.

It took a lot of persuasion to get Mr. Travis to consent to the publication of the facts concerning the strange things that go on inside, outside, and on the roof of his studio. "An old studio, particularly in this great city," said Mr. Travis, "is a rare possession, and as this is one of the oldest to be had in the heart of New York I want it understood that what I shall say is not meant as an adverse criticism of this

ELIZABETH
FOX
OSTERHOUT
FOURTH
CHILD.

delightful old place. On the other hand it really adds to the artistic charm of the place.

"I was on the lookout for this lease a long time before I got it, and two years ago, when Oliver Herford, the author, gave it up I lost no time in closing the deal that made it mine for a period of years. I find it a great pleasure to arrange things to suit myself, and for the first month of my tenancy I spent a large part of the night getting things in order. One of those nights I took particular pleasure in putting in place a Moorish curtain that I prize very highly."

Dog Gave Alarm

"It was about 2 o'clock one morning soon after I moved in that I was hanging this curtain. Buttons, the dog in the story, was sleeping soundly on a divan at the time. Suddenly he jumped down and began to bark savagely. Every hair on his back stood up like quills on a porcupine going into action. The dog ran around the room apparently frightened out of his wits. Then all of a sudden he stopped in his tracks and looked through the door that leads into the room on the Fortieth Street side.

"I thought there was some one in the room and went in there, but it was as silent as a grave. Then I went through every room in the apartment finally opening the door leading into the hallway, and looking down the stairs. No living thing was in sight anywhere. Since that time Buttons has repeated that night's performance at least a dozen times, and to this day the identity of the mythical intruder remains unsolved.

"I am fond of bridge and I have a lot of friends—artists, authors, and actor folk—who like the game also. Every night or two we enjoy ourselves at bridge in this old studio. Like myself, my friends have a fondness for the atmosphere of the place. Sometimes in the midst of our games we all detect a peculiar odor in the air, suggestive of some chemical preparation. We sniff and wonder and then it goes away, to return no more for perhaps weeks, sometimes months. But it always comes back. Where does that odor come from? I don't know; neither do my friends.

An Occult Door

"See that old door with the grill over there? Well, that is one of my prize exhibits. There are two old locks and one new one on the door. The new one has been in place about two years. The old ones have been there for generations, and the keys to them have been lost these many years. You can see how rusty they are. Several months ago I had an engagement to take luncheon with a man with whom I had a business matter to discuss. The engagement was for the noon hour, and about ten minutes before that time a model, who had been posing for me, bade me good-day and started to leave.

"The young woman got to the door and turned the knob, but the door would not open. Then I took a hand and pulled and tugged, but it would not open. I called for the janitor. He came, and pulled and pushed and tugged without avail. The he passed in through the panel some screwdrivers, a hammer, and a hatchet. While I was learning to be a carpenter my business friend came up. He stayed outside and waited for me to finish the job, and, as he had other business to attend to, he fumed and fretted over the enforced delay. Finally the door was taken down, and when we looked at those old locks, rusty with age and unused in years, we found that the bolts in both of them stuck out for an inch. Now, who had locked that door?

"There is an old bell also on that door that is about as old as the locks. Press the button and notice how hard you have to press it to make the bell ring. Well, I may be wrong, but there have been occasions when the bell has rung as many as three times in one day, yet there was not a living person within yards of it at the time. The ringing of the bell invariably follows what sounds like the footsteps of a man ascending the stairs. Buttons goes wild when he hears these mysterious steps, while my models turn pale and some of my male friends feel queer sensations. Really, I wish sometimes that my mysterious friend would introduce himself and settle the mystery of these steps.

"We hear them in other parts of the house also, and at times on the roof. Sometimes there is a clanking noise, as of some one burdened with the ball and chain of servitude, and at other times there is a tinkling sound with them that recalls the legends of ancient shepherds. It is not at all alarming, but it certainly does whet one's curiosity."

Snores in Bathroom

"On several other occasions our attention had been attracted to the bathroom by sounds of loud snoring in there. The snore is that of some giant with lungs of leather. It sounds in the other room as if the snorer might be sleeping in the bathtub. This has happened many times, and on every occasion we investigated, and every time we found the bathroom empty and the tub exactly as we had left it. You see over there a little idol, one of Buddha, that came from Japan. It is made of solid ivory, and there is no mechanism about it. That idol hasn't been moved in months, but on many occasions, sometimes in the night, it emits what sounds like the tick of a great clock. I have gone close to it and put my ear against it and could hear the tick, tick, tick as plainly as I hear your voice. My models and many of my friends have heard it tick, and, like me, they wondered and still wonder where the ticks come from. Old Buddha must have been a funny fellow to have been able to endow a toy like that with the power of making mysterious noises.

"Over the mantel is a painting of 'Circe the Sorceress,' and over there on the wall on the other side of the room are many old swords and knives. One of the knives is a Hindu weapon. Imagine my surprise one morning when I found that knife on the mantel under the painting of "Circe.' How it got there after resting so long on the other side of the room I cannot explain. But that was not all. Right across the breast of 'Circe' there was a long, deep gash, and the gash exactly fitted the edge of the weapon. Explain all these mysteries whoever can."

—*Syracuse Herald*
January 22, 1908

The Holy Name Cemetery can still be visited on Highland Avenue in Otisville.

Alleged Haunted House
Startling Stories Come From Village Of Brookfield

BROOKFIELD- Over in the town of Brookfield, in the southern part of the county, an alleged haunted house is calling forth considerable consideration and discussion, and many conjectures are advanced as to the cause thereof.

Of the situation and the interest excited by the occurrences the Brookfield Courier has the following:

"No little interest has been aroused here during the last few days over some mysterious rappings in a certain house located in the eastern part of our village. The noise, which resembles the muffled striking of a clock, can not be located nor the cause determined. They have been heard by the occupants for the last six months and lately had been getting on their nerves so much that a number have been

called in to hear the noises and assist in an investigation. The rappings have been heard by many and no explanation is forthcoming. The performance begins about 10 o'clock at night and usually last through the night. The programme is about as regular as the Old Faithful geyser but the number of raps varies from three to fifteen at a clip, at intervals of three minutes to a quarter of an hour; but a very strange circumstance is that the number of strokes at which it starts is maintained invariably through the night. Now here is a problem for the thinking machine. Let somebody walk up and solve the mystery. Natural or supernatural? That is the question."
—*Syracuse Herald*
January 17, 1909

Hear Spooks Among Ruins
House At Burks Burned And Aged Woman Disappeared. Foul Crime Two Years Ago. Belief Mrs. Desmond Was Slain, Robbed, And Home Fired To Hide Crime. Weird Noises. Door Bangs Nights, Say Neighbors.

BURKE- Two years ago last August a house was burned in the town of Burke. The owner and occupant, an aged woman, named Desmond, disappeared. It was thought by some that she was burned to death.

It was and is still the opinion of many others, however, that she was murdered and robbed and the house burned to hide the crime. The woman had an insane son. Dennis D. Desmond, now at the State Hospital at Ogdensburg. At the time of the fire, he escaped and reached his home traveling from Ogdensburg afoot. An effort was made to fasten the deed on the son, but he proved an alibi, as the night of the fire he was in or near Valleyfield R.I. Nothing has been seen or heard of his mother since.

Persons living across the road from the ruins of the Desmond house claim the house is haunted, and that spooks occupy the cellar nights, making weird noises and that a certain door in the house opens and shuts after midnight with a bang, but no one is ever seen, and they can't explain the mystery.

—*Syracuse Post Standard*
February 28, 1910

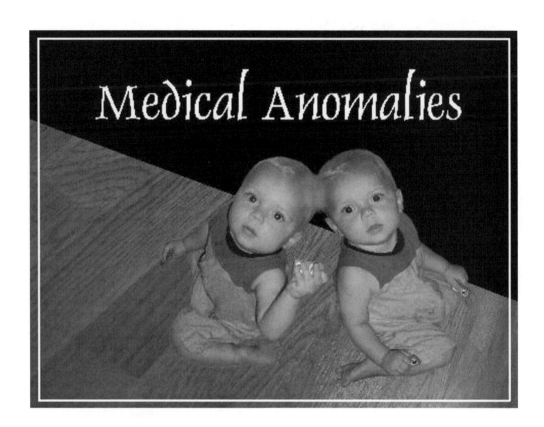

Medical Anomalies

Loses Her Mind
From Grief

CLEBURNE- The wife of one of the negroes killed by lightning about a week ago has become insane, and was found this morning walking about in the graveyard aimlessly calling for him. She is also reported to have been seen walking all over the southern portion of the city in the same manner. Her husband's name was Nathan Crawford, and they had only been married about six weeks.

—*Dallas Morning News*
June 2, 1887

She Was Returned
To Life

A Strange Case Of Resuscitation. At The Door Of The Crematory, Where All Arrangements Had Been Made For Reducing The Body To Ashes.

LONG ISLAND- A living woman for whom the crematory furnace was at its fiercest heat of twenty-seven hundred degrees, Fahrenheit, and for whom the alum sheet was already prepared, is with her husband and children, although on Thursday last she lay in her coffin in a room adjoining the vault where incineration is done. It is a case most horrible to think of or contemplate, and will evident the need of still more stringent laws to govern this new feature in sanitary welfare. Ex-Coroner Hughes is president of the Mount Olive Crematory Association, which, in the form of a Grecian temple, is located in a lovely garden spot at Fresh Pond, Long Island. Dr. Hughes vouches for the correctness of the story, but withholds the name of the physician who made out and signed the death certificate and that of the lady. In the former case he gave his promise only after the most urgent appeals, and then he only consented to keep the story until the annual report is published in October, when his obligations as president of the crematory makes it necessary for him to print the facts, and even then, out of motives of consideration that prevail in every man's breast, he will suppress the name of the unfortunate, yet at the time happy, family that had

The Dead Restored To Life

On the day mentioned a casket containing the body of a woman arrived at the crematory. It came from Fifth Avenue, not far from the Hotel Windsor. Accompanying it was the widower, children and a half dozen relatives. The casket was carried into the reception room, and by its side was placed a costly silver urn, in which ashes were to be subsequently places for final keeping. After a simple service the lid of the coffin was removed and the mourners, one by one, took a last tearful look. The lid was replaced and the floral emblems were again placed in the coffin.

The widower and weeping children were led away to the carriages, and the dead was left to the crematory assistants for incineration. When they were gone President Hughes and his men removed the entire lid and then sent them to prepare the alum

sheet for enveloping the body and to swing the chilled steel cradle into position before

The Glowing Furnace Doors

While they were absent President Hughes turned to a small mirror, and while arranging his tie he was startled by a faint voice at his back, saying "Where am I?" Turning quickly he saw the woman sitting bolt upright in her casket, staring directly at him. When he gathered his scattered wits he realized that prompt action was needed, and stepping to her side he said familiarly: "You are with friends." She has already swung her legs out of the casket and was looking in a dazed way at the urn and then at her burial robes. Assisting her out of the coffin and encircling her with one arm, he carefully kept her head turned from her resting place and half led, half carried her to a cheerful bedroom overhead, occupied by the superintendent and his wife. Soft breezes were coming in the window, and a cheery canary in an alcove sang a song of joy. While the superintendent's wife removed

The Garments Of Death

and put the lady to bed, President Hughes hurried away and returned with some brandy and milk. The drink had the effect of bringing a flush to the cheeks of the patient, succeeded immediately by a quiet doze. The telegraph was brought into requisition, and the husband was soon back at the crematory with a set of his wife's apparel. While he was yet on the way his wife awakened from her nap and asked, "Whose clothes am I wearing?" They were those of a crematory, but that fact was ingeniously concealed in the reply, which seemed to satisfy her. The severest task was when the husband arrived, when they tried to school him into self-control for the interview. The course of procedure agreed upon was carried out to the letter. The husband went into the room with the usual inquiry as to how she felt, and she said if she considered herself strong enough they would return to the city; that in his opinion she had stayed long enough in the country; acquiescing in everything, although somewhat mystified, she arose, dressed herself and announced that she was ready. The husband was now in a tortured frame of mind for he

Dreaded Passing The Front Door

where in large letters was the word "Crematory." The shock of the discovery he feared would kill his wife. Happily, there was a rear door, and through this he led her to a close carriage, and thence, regardless of the fact that there was no road, he had the carriage driven straight across the lawn and field until kindly trees hid the crematory from sight. The he took the smooth pike to the nearest railroad station and a train thence home.

The children had been forewarned of what had occurred, but as an additional precaution they were sent home and were not allowed to see their mother until to-day. She was given to believe that they were away on a visit to New Jersey. The lady's death was attributed to heart disease, and the doctor's certificate to this effect is on file on the health office.

—*Dallas Morning News*
July 24, 1887

EXTRA! EXTRA!

The fear of being buried alive was so prevalent that devices were invented and patented to insure a safe burial. One strange device was a spring loaded casket lid that could be opened by the slightest movement from inside the coffin.

The Sleeping Beauty
She Has Gone To The Other Extreme And Is Now Wakeful

BUFFALO- "The sleeping beauty," Mrs. Emma Althouse, who has been puzzling the doctors and scientists for the last three years, has undergone a wonderful change in her condition. Wakefulness has succeeded the trances which used to last from three to thirty-seven days. The change began to manifest itself about two weeks ago. The periods of slumber gradually decreased in time from an average of eighteen to twenty-five days until her trance lasted only a day at a time, when her condition became normal. Now the periods of sleep are steadily decreasing and she remains awake for forty-eight hours at a time, sleeping about four hours at the end of that time. What the outcome will be cannot be predicted.

—*Dallas Morning News*
July 1, 1890

Levy's Fearful Vision
It Was Only A Synagogue Janitor After All.
Frightful Result Of A Church Keeper Getting Out Of Bed To Close A Window Left Open.

NEW YORK- Moses Levy, a furrier, 26 years of age, who resided at No. 36 Henry Street, was sent to Gouverneur Hospital last night violently insane. Levy had a wife and some children. He resided with them on the second floor of the rear tenement of the above number. The Hebrew synagogue Sharrai Zedeck stands next door to the house in which Levy lived.

About two months ago Levy was awakened out of sleep somewhere near midnight by an unusual disturbance. His bedroom windows face some of the windows of the synagogue, so that while he lay in bed he could see them. On this particular night when Levy was startled from his slumber his eyes fell upon one of the windows of the church and instantly the blood seemed to congeal in his veins and he grew as cold as ice.

There in the synagogue window, which was raised, he saw an awful white figure, seemingly beckoning toward him. To his startled vision the specter-like form was of ominous moment to him. Only for an instant was he apparently an inanimate thing. The trance was removed and he sprang from his bed with a wild shriek, which sent terror into the hearts of his wife and little ones and half of the tenants in the house.

For a long while he could not be calmed down, such a fright had he sustained, when he lad been assured by friends that that which he had seen was no more than a janitor of the synagogue closing the shutters of one of the windows which he had by error neglected to shut after the service of the night. Omitting to perform the duty, he had arisen in the night and rectified the mistake while clothed in his night robe. To the man Levy this experience has proven well nigh fatal to his reason. Since the terrible night he has been afflicted with insomnia. The only sleep which he could seem to obtain was filled with visions of the dreadful specter that he saw on the eventful night.

Morning, noon and at bed time he was continually haunted by the ghoulish presence which occupied his troubled brain. At the workshop he was disturbed and could not attend his duty. There seemed to be no rest for him, no release from the torment. Last night he was seized with a terrible spasm of fear and ran shrieking around his rooms, frightening his wife and filling the children with an unspeakable terror. Policemen Goodwin and Kelly, of the Madison Street station, were called in and took in the insane man to Gouverneur Hospital. All the while he prayed that some one would protect him from the evil thing which was continually trying to kill him. The poor unfortunate fellow will be removed to Bellevue Hospital for treatment to-day.

—*Dallas Morning News*
November 13, 1892

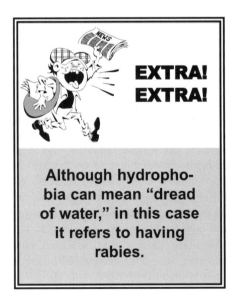

Although hydrophobia can mean "dread of water," in this case it refers to having rabies.

Barks Like A Dog
Terrible Case Of Artist Frank Gregory Of New York

NEW YORK- Frank Gregory, an artist, was bitten by a mad dog three weeks ago, and had developed hydrophobia of a violent type. All his actions and symptoms were identical with those of a dog suffering from a pronounced form of the disease, and those members of the medical profession who saw the patient characterized it as a phenomenal case.

Gregory, who is a painter of portraits and landscapes, is 30 years old. He went to Brooklyn yesterday afternoon to paint a woman's portrait. He was walking along Noble Street, in Brooklyn's Eastern district, shortly after 2 o'clock, when he stopped suddenly at the corner of Franklin Street and put his hands to his head. The he began to wail in a low tone, and people in the street who had noticed his peculiar actions were startled to see him throw himself on his hands and knees and begin to creep rapidly along the sidewalk. His wailing had increased to a prolonged, dismal howling, just such a sound, one of the physicians described, "as a big dog makes sometimes when it sees a full moon rise." People ran from all directions, and, as they pressed about the man on his knees, he changed his howling into a deep bating, as of a hound in full cry. This made the people draw back from him hastily in horror, and then they noticed that his clothes were flecked with foam, which came from his mouth.

Attacks A Little Girl

Shouts that a raving maniac was at large spread and soon five hundred people surrounded the spot where the man was laying. His eye glittered strangely at the shocked and terrified faces about him. Without warning he made a leap at a little girl in the front of the crowd and caught the edge of her skirt in his teeth. The child dashed away, screaming with terror, leaving a portion of her dress in his mouth. This he tore to fragments with his teeth and then set up a terrific barking.

Two policemen pushed through the crowd and seized him by the coat collar, one on each side of him. Like a flash he turned his head and snapped his teeth at the hand of one of the policemen, who let go not a whit too soon. Then the man bit at the other policeman's hand, which was withdrawn just in time to escape his teeth, which snapped together like castanets.

"Look out, he is loose!" yelled a man in the crowd, and there was a wild scattering on all sides as each person sought safety in flight. But the policemen threw themselves upon him and pinned his arms behind his back. All this time the unfortunate maniac kept up a sonorous barking, of about the timbre of a bark of a big Newfoundland dog.

He Barked And Howled

The policemen lifted the man into the ambulance, while he barked and howled lustily. In the ambulance were Surgeons Reilly and Schmidt. Reinforced by two policemen they started the Wildman off to the Eastern District hospital. The surgeons, both stout young fellows too, needed the assistance of the policemen, for the victim of the dog's bite almost succeeded in escaping from the ambulance before it reached the hospital. It was only by the exercise of plenty of muscle that they kept the man from hurling himself headlong into the street.

It took the combined efforts of six men to put Gregory to bed at the hospital. They put his Derby hat by the bed and while they were strapping him down he seized it in his teeth and bit a big hole in it. With the utmost difficulty Surgeon Reilly succeeded in administering some morphine to the sufferer, but it had little effect, for the sick man kept up a fearful racket, barking and baying like a whole pack of foxhounds. After more soothing medicine had been given to him he quieted down for two minutes, the surgeons sat, and gasped out that his name was Frank Gregory, that he was an artist, and lived in Second Street, New York. He said that he had been bitten by a mad dog in Mount Vernon three weeks ago. Then he asked for water.

Chased By A Real Dog

The instant it was brought to him he went off into more violent paroxysms than had yet seized him. His neck seemed to swell up and he appeared to be hocking. The surgeons tried in vain to pour some water down his throat, but their patient became so violent, that they had to desist. The poor fellow's yells and barking disturbed all the patients in the building and threw them into great excitement. The noise was heard a block away and people ran to the

HIDDEN HEADLINES of NEW YORK

hospital in crowds.

Therefore the hospital authorities decided to remove the patient to the Flatbush asylum. He was carried down and put into an ambulance and strapped down to a mattress. He barked and howled all the way to the asylum while a large crowd ran after the ambulance with its strange patient. At the city line, near Prospect Park, a big black dog heard Gregory barking and ran after the ambulance barking loudly. Gregory heard the animal and returned his own noise. The ambulance had to be stopped while the surgeons persuaded some men to drive back the dog, for they feared the patient would strangle with excitement in the ambulance. When the asylum was reached the scenes in the hospital were repeated. The physicians there entertain no hope of Gregory's recovery.

—*Syracuse Evening Herald*
August 19, 1893

EXTRA! EXTRA!

New York was the first state to require license plates on automobiles.

In Her Coffin Alive
On The Way To The Hearse She Tapped On The Coffin Lid

SPRAKERS- Sprakers, a village of this state, was treated to a first-class sensation yesterday by the supposed resurrection from the dead of Miss Eleanor Markham, a young woman of respectable family, who to all appearances had died on Sunday last. Miss Markham, about a fortnight ago, complained of heart trouble and was treated by Dr. Howard. She grew weaker gradually, and on Sunday morning apparently breathed her last, to the great grief of her relatives, by whom she was much beloved.

The doctor pronounced her dead and furnished the usual burial certificate. Undertaker Jones took charge of the funeral arrangement. On account of the warm weather it was decided that the interment should take place yesterday, and in the morning Miss Markham was put into a casket.

After her relatives had taken a last look on what they supposed was their beloved dead the lid of the coffin was fastened on and the undertaker and his assistant took it to the hearse waiting outside. As they approached the hearse the assistance, James Boyle, cried out, while his knees knocked together and his teeth chattered with terror. He insisted that he heard a noise in the coffin.

"You shut your flannel mouth, will you?" said the undertaker, who, however, did not himself seem in good form. "She is alive as sure as there's a God in heaven!" exclaimed Boyle. "Don't you hear her knocking?" "Let us carry her as far as the hearse anyway," said Jones, "and not create a scene that may be absurd and unnecessary." By this time the relatives got wind of what was passing and peremptorily demanded that the coffin be opened. This was done in short order, and behold, there was poor Eleanor Markham lying on her back, her face white and contorted, and her eyes distended in terror.

"My God!" she cried in broken accents, "Where am I?" "You are burying me alive!" "Hush, child," said Dr. Howard, who fortunately happened to be present, "you are all right. It is a mistake easily rectified." The girl was taken into the house and placed in the bed, fainted away, and while the doctor was administering stimulating restoratives the trappings of woe were removed and the hearse drove away with the desired effect. As it was evident to Dr. Howard that her nerves were suffering from the terrible shock they had received he ordered the doors thrown open and told the girl's mother and immediate friends to stay with her until she had completely recovered and say or do nothing in her hearing or sight that was not cheerful and stimulating, above all, not to refer to the late sensational episode. But this Eleanor would not have. She spoke of it herself and seemed relieved and passed into a refreshing slumber when she had unburdened her mind.

"I was conscious all the time you were making preparations to bury me," she said, "and the horror of my situation is altogether beyond description. I could hear everything that was said to a whisper outside the door and although I exerted all my will power and made a supreme physical effort to cry out, I was powerless. I had read in the New York Sunday Advertiser lately about how the Rev. Mr. Kane died and went to heaven, but felt that my fate was to be burned alive, and the frightful idea was the saving of me, for as I was borne to the hearse I prayed to God for strength, and making another attempt succeeded in tapping on the lid of the coffin. At first I fancied the bearers would not hear me, but when I felt one end of the coffin falling suddenly I knew I had been heard."

Miss Markham is on a fair road to final recovery and what is strange is that the mutterings of the heart that brought on her illness are gone.

—*Dallas Morning News*
July 17, 1894

EXTRA! EXTRA!

Adirondack Park is so large that you can combine Yellowstone, Yosemite, Grand Canyon, Glacier, and Olympic National Parks you will still not be as big as it.

Cigarettes Make A Lunatic

A Twenty-year-old Girl Driven Insane By Excessive Smoking

NEW YORK- Cigarette smoking has wrecked the mind of Mamie King, only 20 years old, who but a short time ago was a bright and pretty girl. Now she sits in a cell at the East One Hundred and Twenty-sixth Street police station, a lunatic, with pitiful lack luster eyes. She will go to the Bellevue Hospital insane pavilion to-day and thence to a lunatic asylum, perhaps to spend the balance of her days staring into vacancy and jabbering meaningless sentences. That is what cigarette smoking has done for Mamie King.

The girl lived with her father, Peter King, in a flat at No. 433 East One Hundred and Twentieth Street. There, every minute she wasn't working she had a cigarette in her mouth. If she woke in the night and could not find cigarette she became almost hysterical. The climax was reached yesterday, when the girl locked herself in her room with a package of cigarettes. By and by the father could hear her jabbering to herself. The he tried to induce her to open the door, but she said she would throw herself through the window into the air shaft if he did not go away. He hurried to the station house and asked for help, saying he believed the nicotine poisoned girl would commit suicide if she were not restrained.

Policeman Drumm was sent to the house. He called to the girl to open the door. "Go away!" she screamed. "Let me alone! I'll jump out if you bother me!" Drumm went into the adjoining flat and there found a window overlooking the room in which the girl was raving. Without making any noise he climbed out and reached her window. When she saw the officer she made a frantic effort to jump out, and gave the policeman a fierce struggle. Cigarettes, however, had sapped her strength, and she was finally subdued and taken to the station house in a patrol wagon. On arriving there the first thing she asked for was a cigarette.

"She has smoked for a long time," said her father. "Nothing I could say had any effect upon her. The more cigarettes she used the more she wanted. She was a strong healthy girl, who would have made some man a good wife, before she acquired that awful habit. Cigarettes are worse than whisky. If the girl had been a drunkard she would not have lost her reason so quickly. Whenever I see a man with a cigarette in his mouth I feel like taking it away from him and telling him what a weak, wretched fool he is."

—*Dallas Morning News*
July 30, 1899

Bodies Found Petrified
Result Of Peculiar Properties Of Soil In Cemetery

HANNIBAL- Two bodies which have recently been disinterred for removal from the cemetery here, have been found to be petrified. The last body exhumed was that of Mrs. Rose Vanhorn, who died in 1896. When the sexton opened the grave he found that the coffin had fallen to pieces, but the woman's body was perfectly preserved and the wide-open eyes added to its lifelike appearance.

The doctor who issued the permit to open the grave declared it a remarkable case of petrifaction. "The preservation was just as nearly perfect as it was possible for it to be," he said. "Every vein noticeable in life could be seen. The finger nails were perfect. The most peculiar feature was the eyes. They looked precisely like those of a living person.

"The body was of about the hardness of chalk, but a few years more would have made it as hard as flint. I presume the petrifaction is due to some peculiar quality of the soil." The residents believe that all the bodies interred in the cemetery have undergone a like process.

—*Dallas Morning News*
November 28, 1903

New York State's first capital was Kingston.

Man With Celluloid Nose
Mysterious Patient In Harlem Hospital Who Is Debarred The Pleasures Of Smoking

HARLEM- Physicians in the Harlem Hospital do not like to think of what would happen to one of their patients if he should in a moment of thoughtlessness, attempt to light a cigar. He has been cautioned against such a rash act, as the surgeons are of the opinion that such a proceeding would be attended with unpleasant consequences. He has an artificial nose of celluloid.

Up to the present time they have been unable to figure out a fireproof device to protect the patient from harm in the event of flames coming near him. How the man came to lose his nose is a secret he guards well. Known only as John Doe, he has been under treatment at the institution for an affliction of the remaining section of his proboscis. Pretending to be hard of hearing, he has successfully parried all the surgeons' questions concerning himself and he has become known at the hospital as "the man of mystery."

In the matter of dress the man differs from the usual patient at the dispensary. His clothing is of good quality and he seems to be in prosperous circumstances. At various times he has shaken off the reticence that is one of his characteristics and he had told the surgeons enough to convince them that he comes from a wealthy family. He intimated that the reason he selected the hospital for treatment was because his friends were unlikely to discover him there, as the institution is situated in an out-of-the-way quarter. He visits the hospital for treatment at regular intervals.

"The man is a puzzle to us all," said one of the surgeons yesterday. "He keeps his secret well, and none of us has been able to learn anything about him. I gather from the bits of information that he has told that he was once an inveterate smoker. I believe he lost his nose as a result of a dog's bite. He has admitted that the celluloid nose deprives him of the enjoyment of a smoke, a detail which he keenly deplores. If the man should attempt to light a cigar with the contrivance on his face it would be disastrous. We have cautioned him against such an act of folly."

—*Dallas Morning News*
June 5, 1904

Crazed By Lightning
Woman Struck By Bolt Found Wandering Miles Away

HUNTINGTON- Thrown into a fit of aphasia by a flash of lightning last Sunday, Josephine Donahue of Brooklyn was found wandering aimlessly about the streets of Huntington, L.I., many miles from her home in Brooklyn. Meantime the police of Prospect Park had been dragging the lakes for her body and a general hunt about the city had been instituted.

Miss Donahue, who is 38 years old, was listening to a band concert in the park when the storm suddenly broke. A bolt of lightning struck a tree nearby and the woman leaping from a bench where she sat with her father, ran shrieking through the park. She was soon lost to view and a constant search during four days had produced no trace of her.

How she reached the Long Island town is a mystery. From what can be learned the woman ran through the park in the downpour of rain, boarded a trolley car and later changed to a steam train, which carried her far from the scene where she had been stricken.

—*Dallas Morning News*
August 6, 1905

Mysterious Creatures

A Petrified Giant

To The Editor Of *The Herald*:
This afternoon I visited a farm near Cardiff to obtain from personal inspection all that would be of any use to you relating to the petrified giant which has been discovered there. The fossil was found about three feet below the surface, while digging for a well. The soil is a sort of bluish clay, mixed with quicksand and black iron, and contains about the body specimens of organic remains. The giant lies in a very easy and natural position, horizontal, partly on the right side, with the right hand placed on the bowels, the left as though once lying on the hip and afterwards falling off by his back. Everything so far as discovered, is in a complete state and entire.

The petrified substance seems to be silicate of lime, the crystals being beautifully arranged. The dimensions that I took were – Crown of head to hollow of foot, 10 feet 2 ½ inches; crown of head to tip of chin, 1 feet 9 inches; length of nose, 6 inches; width of nostrils 3 ½ inches; width of mouth, 4 inches; point to point of shoulder, 3 feet; point of hip to knee joint, 3 feet; diameter of calf of leg, 9 ½ inches; diameter of thigh, 1 foot; length of foot, 1 foot 7 ½ inches; width of palm, 7 inches; diameter of wrist, 5 inches.

It has been visited to-day by hundreds from the surrounding country and examined by physicians, and they assert, positively that it must have been once a living giant. The veins, eyeballs, muscle, tendons of the heel and cords of the neck are all very fully exhibited. Many theories are advanced as to where he lived and how he came there. The organic remains in the soil defeat the idea of his antediluvian origin, unless some more recent period the accumulation of ages were washed away and replaced by more modern deposits. There is a large creek, but a few rods from it and but a very little lower, the land being low and wet around it. Mr. Newell proposes now to allow it to rest as found until examined by scientific men. It certainly is one of the connecting links between the past and the present races, and of great value.

—*New York Herald*
October 20, 1860

❖ ❖ ❖

That Sea Serpent In Lake Ontario Once More

SODUS POINT- A correspondent of the Rochester Union & Advertiser, writing from Sodus Point, N.Y., Aug. 7, tell the following:

"Considerable excitement prevails here at the discovery of a veritable sea serpent just outside the piers at the harbor entrance. Some men employed on the public works saw the monster some days ago and reported it, but it was thought they were mistak-

en. Others saw it afterward; and yesterday four or five men in a boat came full upon it, riding the crest of the wave, its head elevated, they say, several feet above the water, and its huge form entirely visible near the surface. They described it as about thirty feet long and as large around as a man's body, resembling as it lay on the water, the 'Liberty pole,' which is of those dimensions. As they rowed after the creature its head descended into the water, and it glided near the surface for some time, affording them a good view till, alarmed at their approach, it plunged down, disappearing in the depths. Efforts will be made to capture it alive for exhibition, but there seems not much chance of its being secured by a hook, and a net could hardly go deep enough. There can be no doubt now, however of the existence of such prodigious serpents in the lake."

—*New York Times*
August 12, 1867

❖ ❖ ❖

Sea Serpent Spotted

NEW YORK- It appears that the sea serpent had now been seen enjoying a quiet and harmless cruise in the placid waters of Newark Bay; but, as on all prior occasions, the story of his appearance had been received with many shrugs expressive of the general incredulity. Notwithstanding the excellent character of many of the witnesses produced, the unfortunate monster is still ruled out for lack of evidence, and declared to be an impossibility of the sea. It is not a little singular that mankind can be brought to believe in all most anything but the sea serpent.

—*New York Times*
July 31, 1869

inquires the remains of which will be embodied in the formal report of the scientific investigation, soon to be given to the public.

—*New York Herald*
November 6, 1869

EXTRA! EXTRA!

Today the Cardiff Giant rests for all to see in the Farmer's Museum of Cooperstown.

Raising Of The Onondaga Giant
Scientific Men Still Wonder Struck

CARDIFF- The Cardiff stone giant was this afternoon successfully raised from the place where it was discovered and brought to Syracuse. It was found to be as perfect on the back, on which it had laid on its clay bed, as on the surface first exposed to view. Professor Hall and Dr. Woolworth were present, and declare the wonder increases in interest the more known of it. They are collecting data and prosecuting

Cardiff Giant

CARDIFF- It is too bad that the Cardiff Giant was discovered to be a humbug so soon. There is no telling to what extent the advancement of science might have been carried had the discovery been postponed, Mr. C. W. Newell, who admits that he was the father of Mr. Cardiff, says: "If Hull (the business manager) hadn't made a d—d fool of himself I should have had the mother of the giant dug up near the same spot soon after the first discovery. There are people in Onondaga to-day who believe that that carved block of gypsum lived and walked where they now live and walk. I intended to have the mother made of plaster of paris, iron and bone, and to have it appear that she had killed herself while defending herself against a large serpent."

—*Cleveland Plain Dealer*
March 25, 1870

Wild Man Discovered
Near New Hampton, N.Y.

NEW HAMPTON- A wild man has been discovered near New Hampton, Orange County, who is creating quite an excitement in that vicinity. A few days ago a party of gentlemen were out shooting along the Big Ditch, a stream which flows through the town, when their attention was attracted by a strange being in a nude state, with long hair and a wild appearance, who appeared to be a man who had been living wild for some time, and who probably has been living in the mountains. He was apparently busy in the destruction of frogs and snakes, and when he observed the party he set up a fierce yell and fled for the woods. A small party gave chase, but was unable to ascertain his whereabouts. He has since been seen by several of the citizens of Dolsentown, but he manages to keep always at a distance. It is probable that he is an escaped lunatic.

—*New York Times*
August 7, 1870

Sea Serpents Seen by The Sea Serpent

NEW YORK- Capt. White of the ship Sea Serpent, which arrived at this point yesterday, reports that on the outgoing passage from New York to China, in latitude of 29° 28' 8?, longitude 170° 45', his attention was called, on the 5th of May, by the seamen on the foretopsail, to a large sea serpent passing within six feet of the ship's quarter.

When the serpent was some fifteen or twenty feet ashore, he lifted his head above the water, opened his mouth, and looked around after the ship with apparent surprise. As near as Capt. White could judge, the serpent must have been fifty feet long and two feet in diameter, and of a deep brown color. About three minutes afterward another of the same species was passed on the other side of the ship within fifteen feet. He was coiled up, and had the appearance of being asleep.

—*New York Times*
January 19, 1873

Freak Of A Colt

PEMBROKE- A few days since J. W. Keen, of Pembroke, N.Y., took his mare from the barn, leaving a two-months old colt behind. On his return some two hours after, he found the colt on the roof of the barn. Being unable to follow the mare, it had sought some means of escape. In the first place it had gone up a flight of stairs—fifteen steps—then over the hay mow, and out a window in the gable end of the barn on to a half-roof. From this elevation it worked its way to the roof of the main barn, which is very steep; then it retraced its steps to the half-roof, whence on the return of the mother it jumped to the ground, a distance of fourteen feet, a feat which it accomplished without being the least injured.

—*Port Jervis Evening Gazette*
October 30, 1873

In 1897, the first Saranac Lake Winter Carnival was held.

A Lurus Natura
A Cat With A Rat's Tail

PORT PERVIS- Joe Zahn, the Opera House saloonist, is the proprietor of a queer freak of nature. He has a very pretty and playful white cat to which is attached a most peculiar candal appendage. Her tail is unmistakably a rat's tail, and the cat seemed to realize a certain sense of degradation and self-abasement in consequence. She is extremely fond of being petted, but when her tail attracts attention she will at once endeavor to scamper off and hide from observation.

—*Port Jervis Evening Gazette*
April 27, 1876

Another Cardiff Giant— As It Were
An Image Of A Man Found In Taughanock Ravine, Tompkins County.
Is It A Petrifaction, Or It Is A Fraud?

ULYSSES- Taughanock Ravine has disgorged a specimen of the genus homo which seems to savor of the long-forgotten past. A man who sported one club-foot, and one other which was inconveniently long, has been torn from his resting place and lies exposed to the mercy of sightseers who have the curiosity and the necessary cash. His stately form when in life must have towered up towards the stars at least six feet and one-half. The length in its present position is six feet and two inches. The shoulders are twenty inches broad.

Dr. Congdon, formerly of the Binghamton Inebriate Asylum, and many other professional men, have examined the specimen to-day. No one seems willing to express an opinion about the matter, and in fact the mystery is great. If it is not a genuine petrifaction, it is certainly an excellent fraud. The circumstances attending its discovery are perfectly natural, and to all appearances there is no bad faith about it. The hands are crossed at the wrists and the left leg crosses the right midway below the knee. The appearance of the body leads to the belief that the individual was on earth before our present civilization and must have belonged to a people now extinct.

His remains were discovered by the roadside on the north bank of the Taghanic Ravine and some distance above the Falls. About three feet of earth covered the body, and the remains of a stump indicate that he was buried at the foot of the tree. The stump was decayed and gone clear below the surface of the ground, and only a trace of it remains. Mr. John M. Thompson, the owner of the "fossil," has been improving the upper part of the glen for some time, and workmen in his employ found the specimen.

—*The Cuba Patriot*
July 11, 1879

Human Monstrosity At Nobody's

NARROWSBURG- A curious specimen of humanity exists at Nobody's station, west of Narrowsburg, in Sullivan County.

It is a male, 22 years of age, and has the use of neither his limbs nor his reason. His weight is less than 25 pounds. This being looks more like a large sized baby than a man. The father says that shortly before the child was born a monkey jumped into an open window and terribly frightened the mother. The child was born in England.

—*Port Jervis Evening Gazette*
August 2, 1879

Saw A Sea Serpent
The Awful Effects Of
Not Drinking Water

UNION SPRINGS- A New York salesman, suffering from a terrible attack of the jim-jams produced by too much ingestion to the other contents of Cayuga Lake as a beverage, wrote the Sun an account of a huge sea serpent he saw sea-sawing through the neglected fluid of that lake. He and his companion took refuge on an island near Sheldrake (there being but one island in the lake, opposite Union Springs) and the awful monster dived down into subterranean passage and returned thereby to the ocean via the Panama Canal without stopping at Monte Ruma.

—*Syracuse Morning Standard*
July 14, 1880

New York's Dead Whale
The Singular Discovery Made In The Mouth Of A Huge Fish

NEW YORK- Between sixty and seventy barrels of cork chips and several barrels of embalming fluid now lying at the foot of Stanton Street that had formerly been occupied by the stomach, liver, heart, and other portions of a whale's anatomy known under the general name of "innards." These portions of the huge fish were not rendered available for exhibition purposes and so they were removed and the cork substituted. This will have a tendency also to do away with the possibilities of decomposition. The removal has not resulted in banishing the peculiar odor that attaches to a whale, however, and one which largely discounts anything that Communipaw has ever done, and is a fair rival to Hunter's Point odors. It took three good sized wagons to carry away the lover of the whale, and its heart made one full wagon load and nearly half of another. Naturalists, and ichthyologists in particular, may be interested in knowing that.

Whales Are Numbered

This fact has not been revealed until now, and scientists can quarrel over this peculiar freak of nature and give theories to an admiring and wondering world. The discovery that this whale is numbered was made on Thursday, when the mouth of the mammoth was being washed out with a few barrels of disinfecting fluids. On the right side of the lower jawbone, where the tongue is attached to it, the figures 127 could be plainly discerned standing out in pale pink color, and rather irregularly defined on the dark background where these figures. How they come there and why they are there is a question that is just now agitating the minds of the captors. One of them, an old whaleman, says he never noticed anything of the kind before, probably because he never before critically examined a whale's mouth. The figures could not have been made there by anyone, for they are in that portion of the jaw which a workman could not get at to cut them there. A Brooklyn physician who believes in embalming has applied for and obtained permission to embalm the huge fish.

—*Syracuse Herald*
March 26, 1882

That Mermaid

SYRACUSE- Two Herald reporters paid five cents each last night to see "the most wonderful curiosity on earth, the Chinese Mermaid," as it was announced on a hand-bill, which also contained a picture of a well developed young woman with a large fish's tail. The inquisitive young men found a glass case about eighteen inches long by perhaps eight in width and height, which contained something that looked like a cross between a monkey, a lizard, and a fish.

—*Syracuse Herald*
March 26, 1882

A Sea Serpent
Graphically Described
By A Sea Captain

NEW YORK- Capt. A. H. Smith, from the schooner E. H. Harriman which arrived a few hours ago, after a twelve days voyage from (not readable) reports that the vessel meet a genuine sea serpent on the fourth day out. The captain says "In latitude 31 degrees and 10 minutes, longitude 71 degrees and 30 minutes I saw what at first I thought to be a school of whales, but by close observations I knew it was some other great thing. It was coming toward me without (not readable) and with more than railroad speed. It came up from leeward and as soon as it got within half a mile of us it sank an again (not readable) its appearance two miles to windward. I now discovered that it was a sea serpent with three large bumps on his back about

seventy-five feet apart. The whole serpent must have been at least three hundred feet long, of black color and is (rest of article not readable)

—*Fort Wayne Sunday Gazette*
October 11, 1885

Serpent Seen

DEMSTER- A few days ago according to a correspondent of the Oswego Palladium, David Wiggins and Ad Button saw a sea serpent or something like it at Demster Beach, east of Oswego. It came near the shore of the lake and ran its head up from the water four or five feet, and was about the size of a six inch stove pipe.

—*Syracuse Daily Standard*
April 30, 1886

Our Old Friend
The Sea Serpent

NORFOLK- The sea serpent has made its appearance hereabout. Last night it was seen off Ocean View by a number of reliable people, who say that his head resembled that of a horse, and that a row of serrated protuberances ornamented the upper portion of the head. Owing to the indistinct sight at the time the length of the serpent could not be determined but it is variously estimated by those who saw it to be about 130 feet in length and of a dull gray color. It remained on the surface about five minutes, then disappeared beneath the water, emitting a peculiar whistling noise resembling the sound of escaping steam.

—*New York Times*
August 12, 1886

Sea Serpent

KINGSTON- The sea serpent has become tired of the hot weather along the coast, and following the example of the early Dutch navigation he is on his way up the Hudson River in the hope of finding a northwest passage to a cooler place. Some boys who were swimming near Kingston on Sunday saw the head and about three feet of the dirty white neck of the monster; but like the king of beasts the sea serpent is said to be most terrible when "A lashing of his tail," and the latter act was performed in the same vicinity. It is suspected that the serpent had heard of the President's poor luck at fishing and that his ultimate destination is Saranac Lake by way of Champlain Canal. Fish stories from the Adirondack's may be expected to grow in size and interest before leaves begin to turn.

—*Syracuse Daily Standard*
August 31, 1886

Personal Information

NEW YORK- Detective Harvey is after a red-tailed sparrow. He has noticed him several times in City Hall Park. Mr. Harvey had two theories about the sparrow. One is that the creature lighted on a roof freshly painted red and besmeared his tail. This is the most occult explanation and finds favor with Chief Wright. Mr. Harvey's other theory is that the sparrow is a phenomenon, a freak of nature.

—*Syracuse Herald*
October 31, 1886

Sees Sea Serpent

LONG ISLAND- Captain Sherman of the schooner Coral asserts that last Friday, while his craft was near Cornfield lightship on Long Island Sound, he and his able and truthful mate saw a sea serpent fully one hundred feet long, as large around as a flour barrel and with a head like an alligator's. The creature was about two hundred feet away when first observed, and moved rapidly away towards the mouth of the Connecticut River. The serpent is evidently on a cruise for shad.

—*Syracuse Evening Herald*
March 30, 1888

Monster Sea Serpent Seen In Owasco Lake

Well Known Men Declare The Reptile Exists.
An Old Legend Is Revived And Evidently Believed In Auburn.

AUBURN- About two years ago several fishermen who frequent Owasco Lake declared that a large sea serpent existed in that body of water. They had seen him and were positive in their assertions.

The matter was forgotten until recently. Now the claim is made by Fred C. Hayden and James O. Thomas that they have seen the monster.

Dove To The Bottom

The two men were trolling near Buck's Point yesterday afternoon, when they noticed a long, dark object in the water some yards away. The object, which at first was thought to be a tree trunk, was moving against the wind and waves. In order to get a better view of the object the two men stood up in the boat, only to see the monster disappear under the water. Several others whose veracity is not usually questioned claim to have seen the serpent.

—*Syracuse Post Standard*
July 8, 1889

Half Human-Half Monkey
A Strangely Malformed Boy At The Barge Office

NEW YORK- A most remarkable malformed human creature is now detained at the Barge Office. He arrived in this country yesterday on the steamship Kaiser Wilheim II, of the North German Lloyd line. He is the son of John Ginsler, a Hungarian, who is also accompanied by his wife and four other children. The party was practically without funds. Asked where they were going, they said New York. They were taken to the Barge office as persons likely to become public charges, and will, in all probability, be sent back.

The eldest child is named Herrman. A stranger creature has never been seen in the Barge office, where strange creatures are by no means so rare as they are in most places. His mother says that he is 10 years old, but he does not look, judged by his size, to be over 3 years of age. He wears a roughly-made dress, with a long skirt. He was taken into a private room and examined. He seemed as much ape as human.

In the first place, the child's face has all the characteristics of the face of a monkey. The general contour of the head is apelike. The forehead slopes backward and the chin recedes abruptly from the lower lip to the neck. The head is small, there being little difference between the size of it and of the neck. The eyes are sunken in the head and are never at rest. The hair in the center of the forehead reaches down almost to the nose, which is broad and flat, with big, ever dilating nostrils. The mouth is tremendously large, with jaws and teeth sharp and very large. The ears are small and flat.

The trunk of the body is as small as that of a 3-year-old child, but is muscularly developed to an unusual degree. The arms are unusually short and the legs very long, absolutely monkey-like in formation. The boy, if boy he may be called, never stands upright. When moving he jumps along on all fours, after the fashion of a monkey. When at rest he squats like a monkey and beats his breast with his arms, as a monkey does. His hands and feet are very large, and while human in form, have very long fingers and toes and very big joints.

The boy is absolutely without intelligence. He chatters almost continually, as a monkey chatters. His mother says that nobody but herself can understand anything that he articulates, and she only knows a few sounds as expressing his desire for food and drink. He seems to have no understanding except the instinct of the beast.

The father, mother and rest of the family are immigrants of ordinary intelligence as Hungarian immigrants run, and all of the children except this strange creature are bright and rather pretty. Colonel Weber expects that he will be besieged by dime museum proprietors who will want the freak of which he now has custody, but says that they will be disappointed in their desire to secure him.

—*Dallas Morning News*
September 15, 1891

Wooly Bull Calf

MILO- Robert Newby, a resident of Milo, has a curious freak of nature among his live stock. It is a wooly bull calf, and is but two months. The hair is believed to be actual wool and is black in color. There is not a particle of hair on its tail.

—*Olean Democrat*
April 7, 1892

The Warwick Devil
A New York Reporter Come To Orange County To Write Up The Strange Occurrence

WARWICK- The item that first appeared in the Warwick Dispatch, that George Springer, Gode Smith, David Green and Dory Tomer, of Warwick assert that a frightful apparition, believed to be the devil, was seen by them while passing the Warwick Mountain at night, was sent to the New York papers and yesterday a Sun reporter arrived in Middletown to look the matter up. Of course he could get no information in Middletown in regard to the party he was looking for and he was directed to Warwick.

The Warwick parties say the apparition was so terrible in appearance that although the witnesses are possessed of great courage, they made a stampede for home. The apparition is described as having face and hands which shone like a bottle, while the rest of it was black as jet. Even the dogs with the party were as badly frightened as their masters.

—*Middletown Daily Times*
May 27, 1893

Cayuga Lake's Sea Serpent

LUDLOWVILLE- The Journal last week told of the strange actions of an unknown swimmer in Cayuga Lake off Ludlowville the preceding day. It will be remembered that the swimmer was not discovered until about 200 feet from the shore. No one knew who he was, where he started from or how he got in the lake, or was able to get a close view of him. The object looked like the head of a man with a hat on it. It continued swimming out into the lake until lost from sight. This incident was observed by an attaché of The Journal. At the time it was wondered if the supposed man reached the other shore.

Last Wednesday a well-known Ithaca gentleman was on the west shore of the lake hunting, having with him his two hired men. Looking out into the lake he was astonished to see what appeared to be a man with a hat on his head swimming around about 300 feet from shore. The swimmer was apparently tireless, for the three men watched him for fully half an hour. Then a pair of marine glasses were procured, and looking through them the gentlemen saw not a man swimming about, but a large serpent with its head high out of the water. The gentlemen immediately fired at the object, which, at the report of the gun, disappeared from view. The story is certainly true, being vouched for by the three men, and explains the mystery of the strange swimmer of a week ago.

It is a well-known fact that not a summer passes but that this same serpent is seen by some one, but when told of the story is laughed at. Why is it not within the range of possibilities for such an animal to exist in the waters of such a large lake?

—*Syracuse Evening Herald*
September 19, 1894

Roaming The Mountains

MANCHESTER- Manchester township, which lies north of Paterson, a thickly settled agricultural portion of Passaic County, is in the state of excitement over a wild man that is said to be roaming the mountains in the vicinity of Haledon.

Two hunters who saw the man say he is tall, naked and with a shock of matted, red hair. The hunters declare that he is not only a giant in stature, but that he is a perfect Hercules in strength. The maniac crawled over the rocks like a serpent, wriggling his body and digging his feet into the rock to facilitate his movements. The hunters were so badly frightened at the sight of him that they held their breath for fear of alarming him. They saw him make off in the brushwood and take a route leading toward Haledon. It is believed that he is a lunatic that has escaped from either the Middletown or Morristown insane asylums.

—*Syracuse Evening Herald*
October 4, 1894

Has Three Legs
Monstrosity In The Shape Of A Boy At Oswego

OSWEGO- What is considered one of the greatest freaks of nature was born in this city one week ago in the shape of a boy baby with three legs and but one arm. Medical men who have examined the monstrosity say it is certainly a wonderfully marked child, and is the only one of its kind ever born.

The parents who live in West Seneca Street, are very sensitive over the child's misfortune and tried their best to prevent the fact being given to the public, but neighbors who visited the house talked the strange infant over, and it became noised about in that way. The child is in the best of health and doing nicely, and unless something unforeseen happens, will live. But the mother is in a critical condition.

—*Syracuse Sunday Herald*
March 19, 1899

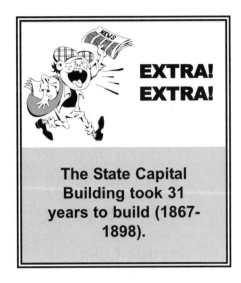

The State Capital Building took 31 years to build (1867-1898).

Real Sea Serpent Is Here At Last
Uncanny Creature A Prisoner In The Aquarium

Sent from Bermuda by Prof. Bristol, who never saw its like and does not know how to class it.

NEW YORK- In tank No. 3 on the south ground floor of the Aquarium, there was deposited yesterday the strangest creature the authorities have even been called upon to take care of. The creature, which may be a snake, or a moray, or a deep sea eel, or a sea serpent, arrived on the Quebec Line steamship Trinidad, and was sent north by Prof. Charles L. Bristol, Professor of Biology in New York University who is at present in Bermuda securing rare piscatorial specimens for the Aquarium.

The creature is about six feet long, has a reptilian head, the body of a moray, and the tail of a fish. Its body is of a rich brown, striped or spotted at regular intervals with beautiful bands and spots of a light yellow. That it is very much alive is shown by its lively movements in captivity. It is on the go all the time, sometimes whirling upward, then down or sideways, striking its head against the glass walls with considerable force when the later movement is indulged in.

Prof. Bristol in his letter to Mr. Spencer said he had no idea what the specimen was and asked that he be informed as soon as the problem had been solved. He suggested that it might be a species of the deep sea eel, but that was only a surmise and he frankly admitted that for once he had run across a fish or reptile the like of which he had neither seen nor heard of before. From another source Mr. Spencer learned the story of the capture of the creature.

"I don't know what it is," began Mr. Spencer, "but whatever it happens to be, it was captured in eleven fathoms of water, about seven miles northeast of Bermuda." The fact that a few feet away from the point of captivity there is a ledge where the water suddenly increases to 200 fathoms in depth probably led to the suggestion from Prof. Bristol that the creature is a species of the deep sea eel.

Three Bermuda negro fishermen made the catch. All were intoxicated at the time, and were about ready to return home when they thought it would be a wise thing to pull in a line that they had set some hours before. One of them grabbed the line and tried to pull it in, but it became taut and refused to give. Thinking the hook had

caught around a piece of coral, another grasped the line, but it still remained secure, and the third man was called on to lend his assistance.

Pull as they would they cold not dislodge the hook. Finally, all their efforts to pull the line clear proving unavailing, they decided to put on the jack ledge which is an iron ring used to ease the hook off. This scheme failing, an attempt was made to break the line and then trouble took place. While they were pulling with all their might the line suddenly eased, and before any of them had a chance to realize what had happened the 'sea serpent' had been pulled out of the water and into the boat.

One of the negroes, a very superstitious fellow, thought the thing was the devil, and cowered in the bottom of the boat praying and yelling for mercy. The other two almost swooned with fright. All three remained this for some time, when one of them, a little braver than the others took a look at the strange catch and as he did not seem to be very vicious, despite his warlike appearance, finally managed to persuade his companions – all three were perfectly sober now – to take up their oars and pull for home.

When they arrived home the story of their catch soon became town talk and a young naturalist of St. George, Prof. Mowbray secured the creature and placed it in a tidal pool for safe keeping. Nothing like it had ever been seen in Bermuda. From Mr. Mowbray Prof. Bristol secured it for the Aquarium. Besides the mysterious creature Prof. Bristol also sent to the Aquarium a lot of fine specimens of tropical fish.

There were many brilliantly colored angel and surgeon fish, a score or so of little silver butterfly fish or 'four-eye' fish, five uncanny spiny Bermuda lobsters, an equal number of funny looking little cowfish and two rainbow tinted ladyfish. In the entire lot, which came in eight tanks, there were twenty-eight varieties totaling 143 specimens.

—*New York Times*
July 1, 1902

Whoppers

NEW YORK- Whoppers about a captive sea serpent are now being circulated in New York. They say it was seven feet long when it was put into the tank, but that it has continued to shrink until it is now about

four feet from tip to tip. The pretty creature is chocolate hued, with cream colored bands and spots and answers to the name of channemuraena vittate.

—*Syracuse Post Standard*
July 4, 1902

Green Goats
With Red Legs
Apparition That Startled People In West Hoboken
And Got A Man Into Trouble

WEST HOBOKEN- Two pea green goats with vermillion legs ambling through the streets of West Hoboken are a daylight apparition which has caused bibulous folk to shudder and pass by with fixed features and blanching cheeks, while others stood and wondered at the sight.

The goats were real, however. They are the property of Paul Crobach, the village blacksmith of Edgewater, but he was as surprised as anyone when they came home in such radiant aspect, and for a time refused to recognize them as his property. At last, however, he knew them by some points of physical contour, and took them in, and they now mope about his grounds.

He set an investigation on foot and it is pretty well established that the goats came to grief through their appetites. Their taste reverted from tomato cans to tomato plants, and they satisfied their hunger upon those that were rapidly approaching the bearing point in the garden of Michael Hawkins, who works in the Ellis Oil

Works. Further stories told about the neighborhood cause Crobach to apply for a warrant for Hawkins' arrest on a charge of cruelty to animals in corralling his goats and painting them in colors that will not wash away.

Hawkins was yesterday held on this charge by Recorder Hinners, who fixed bail at $100. The Society for the Prevention of Cruelty of Animals has taken a hand in the case and will press the complaint.

—*New York Times*
July 20, 1902

EXTRA!
EXTRA!

The New York State Canal System is 524 miles long and has 57 locks.

Lively Lamb
With Two Legs
Handicapped As To Locomotion
But Jeeps Up With The Flock

MALONE- James Traverse, a farmer of South Malone, has a freak of nature among his flocks, the game being a lamb several

months old, evidently in good health, but which was born with only two legs. Though seriously handicapped as to the means of locomotion the lamb manages to travel around with the other sheep and keep up with them, without much difficulty.

—*Syracuse Post-Standard*
October 6, 1902

Topsy, A Very Bad
Elephant,
Poisoned, Electrocuted
And Hanged

BROOKLYN- Topsy, the elephant who killed two men in Texas and a third in Brooklyn borough after he had fed her a lighted cigarette, was electrocuted on Coney Island yesterday, after a vain attempt had been made to entice her across a bridge to a scaffold where she was to have been hanged. When her keeper, "Whitey" Alt, left the employ of Thompson & Dundy, the proprietors of the park, last Friday, Topsy broke loose and made things lively in the thoroughfares of Coney Island. As nobody else could handle Topsy and as the animal's vicious temper did not improve, it was though best to kill her.

Loaded with chains, Topsy lumbered along until she neared the place where it was proposed to hang her. She tried the little bridge that led to it, and apparently scenting danger, refused to go any further, and slowly turned about. She was coaxed with apples, carrots, and hay for nearly two hours, but would not cross the bridge, and the idea of hanging her had to be abandoned. Preparations were then made to kill her by electricity.

It took a long time to get Topsy's feet in the metallic plates, as she was suspicious and shifted uneasy from one foot to the other while she watched the movements of the attendants. She tugged at her chains uneasily, but before she had any chance to display any temper she was quieted with apples and carrots. Finally two electrodes on the boards were securely fastened to one of Topsy's forefeet and to a hind foot. The she was given 200 grains of cyanide of potassium in three carrots and in a moment after she had swallowed the poison the electrician turned in the current and 6,000 volts shot through her.

There was a flash of fire and an odor of burning flesh. The chains rattled and the hawser cracked like whips. Then slowly, like a prize fighter who has received a terrific swing on the jaw, her legs bent under her and she rolled over on the ground. There was no trumpeting of pain or rage. The windlass drew the rope around her neck taut, cutting of her wind and Topsy was officially pronounced dead.

—*Milwaukee Journal*
January 5, 1903

In 2003, a memorial for Topsy was constructed at the Coney Island Museum.

Jaguar That Killed Mate Goes Insane

NEW YORK- The keepers in the New York zoological garden have decided that Lopez, the jaguar that killed his mate some time ago, is insane. At times Lopez will try to climb to the top of his cage, and at other times he barks and growls like a dog.
—*Milwaukee Journal*
January 19, 1903

Marine Monster

NEW YORK- The crew of the Red Dragon, a fishing boat of this port, sighted a marine monster about twenty-five miles off shore the other day, and after a desperate battle succeeded in killing it. It is not a sea serpent, but is as queer a beast as that hackneyed sea shore resort visitor. It has a head similar to that of a calf, with the body of a sunfish, twelve feet in length, and weighing 3,000 pounds. It is totally different from anything ever seen in these waters. It has ears like those of an elephant and was dubbed "elephant fish" by its captors. A detailed description of the monstrosity has been sent to the Academy of Sciences in Philadelphia.

—New York Times
August 23, 1903

Killed A Giant Hawk
It Was Destroying Squirrels
In Central Park.
Keeper Had A Lively Tussle.

NEW YORK- An extremely large red-tailed hawk flew over from the wilds of New Jersey two weeks ago and taking a birdseye view of the city, dropped down into Central Park. It found the foraging there to its liking and stayed. The policeman then began to send in almost daily reports of it depredations among the gray squirrels in various parts of the park.

The hawk had little trouble in catching the squirrels in the snow or on the trees, and is said to have destroyed dozens of them. It

was first reported from the Ramble, where the policeman who saw it surmised from its size that it was an eagle. He so declared in his report to the sergeant at the Arsenal.

Director Smith of the menagerie was notified that a stray eagle was living in the park eating squirrels. The director sent out "Billie" Snyder, the elephant man, with a gun to get the supposed eagle, but the keeper tramped through the park for several days without seeing the bird. Policemen reported it at the block home, then at the North Meadows, and again at the Kinderberg, and the bird grew in size with each report.

Policeman Madigan saw it on Thursday near the Angora goat enclosure in the menagerie. It flew from a tree to the roof of the goat house and made so much noise with its wings that Madison thought a big eagle had got its eye on one of the Angora goats and proposed to carry it off for dinner. He blew his whistle and clapped his hands and it went off toward the Mall.

When Snyder went to the park yesterday morning he caught sight of the hawk perched on the upper ledge of a top story window of the Arsenal. It seemed to be looking down at the elephant house, but Snyder didn't suppose it contemplated trying to carry off any of the inmates. However, he got his gun in a jiffy, and fired at the bird, wounding it.

It flew to the small lawn near the deer paddock, and the keeper dropped his gun and ran and seized the bird. At least, he tried to seize it, but the hawk put up a stubborn fight with wing, talons and beak. The keeper had his fingers cut and the skin on his face was scratched by the flapping of the wings. The two tumbled about on the snow for a time but finally the keeper threw his weight on the bird and held it down until he had squeezed the life out of it. The bird measured five feet from wing tip to wing tip. Director Smith is going to have it mounted and will keep it in his office.

—*Syracuse Herald*
February 20, 1904

Pair Of Wings

BLOOMINGBURG- D. C. Noxon had a two-year-old Jersey heifer, which gave birth to a calf, Wednesday, which was a great freak, the head being the most natural part. It had three hind legs, one front one, with the two in the rear grown over its back toward the neck, the ribs growing over the back like a pair of wings with the stomach exposed.

—*Middletown
Orange County Times-Press*
March 9, 1906

Calf With Six Legs

WATERTOWN- Lyman Warth of Adams Center brought to this city to-day a calf having six legs. The freak attracted lots of attention at the stables in the rear of the Romang House. The extra legs grow out of the shoulders, one on each side, but in all other respects the calf was perfectly

formed. The creature died before it was brought here.

—*Syracuse Post Standard*
April 11, 1906

Freak Cat Wanders Away
Owners Fear Some Horrible Bulldog Might Devour Their Pet

SYRACUSE- Eben, a beautiful black cat possessed of seven toes on each foot has strayed away and the family of Frank P. Carney of No. 103 Midland Avenue is in distress over the whereabouts of their pet.

"We were so afraid that some horrible bulldog might get him that we advertised in the paper for him," said Miss Carey last evening. It is said that bulldogs are plentiful on the neighborhood.

—*Syracuse Post Standard*
May 11, 1906

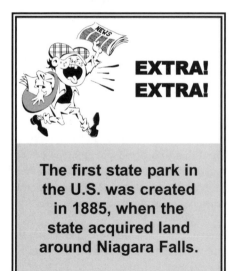

The first state park in the U.S. was created in 1885, when the state acquired land around Niagara Falls.

Lambs Like Turtles
Peculiar Freak Of Nature Noted On A Farm Near Medina

MEDINA- A peculiar freak of nature occurred on the farm of William Guyger, north of Medina last week. Guyger is something of a sheep fancier and has a large flock of blooded sheep. These have always been pastured near a creek flowing through the farm in which there are any number of mud turtles. Now the lambing time has arrived. Guyger is surprised to find that seven or eight ewes have given birth to lambs that resemble mud turtles in many ways. They had long heads with the under jaw projecting out two or three inches beyond the upper jaw, the legs protruding from the sides of the bodies almost parallel with the ground, similar to those of a turtle, while the bodies were round and inclined to be flat.

The resemblance was most striking, and the farmers in that community can conceive of no reason for this freak of nature unless it is from the fact that the ewes were pastured in the field joining the creek and drank from the stream where the mud turtles lived. All of the lambs died within two or three days after they were born.

—*Syracuse Herald*
March 30, 1907

High Bred Cow Gives Birth To A Freak Calf
Face Resembles A Bull Dog And Tail And Legs Are Lacking

TUPPER LAKE- One of the Irish cove which Colonel William Barbour of New York, the linen thread man, imported last summer for his farm on Big Tupper Lake, gave birth to a black calf whose entire body is not much more than a foot long, the head constituting the larger part. The creature had a face resembling an extremely ugly bull dog and has no tail.

Its legs are little more than an inch long, coming out like claws on the sides of the body. The calf was born dead and is now at one of the local drug stores in alcohol, and will doubtless be preserved and stuffed later as a genuine freak.

—*Syracuse Post Standard*
June 5, 1907

Who's The Mother?
A Subtle Question For The Grange To Consider. An Unheard Of Performance.

GRANGE- Alanson Comfort, a well known farmer of Wallkill River Grange, who resides on the Mount Hope Road, near this city, has a freak of nature on his farm which is humorous in the extreme.

A guinea hen had been placed on a setting of eggs and was getting along comfortably and serenely, when a turkey gobbler espied her, and seemed to envy her job.

Accordingly, he drove her from the nest and took possession, the latter part of last week, and has since been performing all the functions of a setting hen. As all who are at all acquainted with poultry know, guinea hen's eggs have very tough shells and it takes them four weeks to hatch. The guinea hen had taken care of the eggs for nearly three weeks, so Mr. Gobbler had quite a spell of duty yet on hand. He clucks and ruffles up his feathers, if approached, after the fashion of a hen, leaves the nest once in a while to get food and then resumes his setting. He has twenty-three eggs under him, and, for the present, at least, is performing much more than his share of hard work in the world, much of it self-assumed.

But this curious performance brings up an interesting question, which the grange can't solve, we'll bet: Who'll be the mother of those chicks, the guinea hen or the gobbler?

—*Middletown Orange County Times*
June 30, 1908

A Fearsome Creature
Eats The Heads Off Pigs And Kills Watchdogs

HAMBURG- A mysterious animal has been killing cattle in the northern section of Berks County during the past week. From the descriptions given by those who caught a glimpse of the strange creature, no one is able to tell just what kind of an animal it is that is doing the damage.

On Tuesday night the beast visited the farm of J. A. Bausher, near Hamburg, tenanted by Harry Faust. The place is located along the base of the Blue Mountains. Mr. Faust was awakened by hearing noises at his pig pen. He hurriedly dressed, and, securing a pitchfork, arrived at the pen just in time to see the animal leap over a fence. According to his account, the killer is as large as a New Foundland dog and has a tail like a wolf.

To his great surprise Mr. Faust found the heads of eight of his small pigs chewed off. A large watchdog belonging to Mr. Faust had also been killed. The creature next visited the farm of Harvey Shollenberger and there killed a watchdog and injured a Holstein calf. The mysterious animal then killed a dog at the farm of Herman Bailey, and at Charles Fink's near by, killed a flock of geese and a large bulldog.

Farmers for miles organized and thoroughly armed started out on a search for the mysterious creature. Traps will be set at night in an effort to catch the monster. A strange feature is that after the animal kills the cattle and dogs it does not devour any portion of the carcass but the head.

—*Olean Evening Times*
June 8, 1909

Canastota Hen Lays Very Remarkable Egg

CANASTOTA- John Roberts had an unusually small game hen, weighing not to exceed two and one-half or possibly three pounds, which has probably laid the largest egg ever produced by a Canastota hen. The egg was laid in a neighbor's barn yesterday, following a rest of three or four days in the part of the hen and was in every respect a monster and freak. It weighed more than half a pound and when accidentally broken was found to contain immediately within the other hard shell an ordinary double-yolk egg. Inside this was another perfectly formed egg of ordinary dimensions surrounded by a perfectly formed hard shell.

—*Syracuse Herald*
September 18, 1909

An Odd Freak

MIDDLETOWN- An odd freak of nature was born on the farm of E. P. Lory last week. It was a calf with two fully developed heads. It lived only a short time.

—*Orange County Times Press*
July 29, 1910

White Deer Shot By A Canton Man On The Granshue
Freak Buck Also Has Peculiarly Shaped Head

CANTON- "Arve" Eastman, a well-known guide and hunter brought in a curiosity yesterday in the shape of a pure white deer. Mr. Eastman, Thomas Cotter and Rufus Allen, all of Canton, were hunt-

ing on the Granshue, when Mr. Eastman shot the animal.

It is a buck, apparently about a year old, and has the appearance of an ordinary deer of that age excepting its color, which is pure white, and the shape of the head, the forehead being somewhat more prominent than is common. White spotted deer are occasionally shot here, a pure white deer is a curiosity, and no one seems to have ever seen one before. Mr. Eastman shipped the hide with head and hoofs to Saranac, where it will be mounted.

—*Syracuse Post Standard*
October 19, 1910

Wolf Bites Women In Brooklyn Theater
Beast Escapes From Enclosure And Leaps Over The Footlights. Officer Subdues Snarling Animal With Club.

BROOKLYN- During the progress of a melodrama in a theater in Brooklyn tonight, a wolf in a wire inclosure on the stage escaped and, jumping over the footlights and into the auditorium, attacked Mrs. Florence Baumgartner and Miss Tessie Verhalter. Both were bitten on the hands. The brute leaped about snapping and snarling.

While the excitement was at its height Policeman Cosgrove entered into the fray and with blows from the night-stick quelled the animal, but not before he also had received a laceration of the hand.

When the wolf had been caged again the show proceeded.

—*Syracuse Post Standard*
December 20, 1910

Stage Wolf Caused Panic
Escaped Into The Audience And Bit Five Woman And Two Men Before It Was Caged. A Policeman Jumped Onto The Animal And Seized It By The Throat. Victims Under Treatment.

WILLIAMSBURG- Five woman and four men were bitten when a big grey wolf broke his cage on the stage of the American Theatre, Williamsburg, and leaped into the audience, are receiving careful medical treatment for fear the wounds may have fatal results.

The wolf threw the 300 persons in the audience into a panic in which many were jostled and bruised. Finally Policeman Cosgrove seized the savage beast by the throat and, though his hand and wrist were bitten, carried the animal back to the stage with the assistance of a stage hand and replaced it in its cage. Those who were bitten had their wounds cauterized by an ambulance surgeon. Pending their recovery the wolf will be placed under observation.

The wolf and his mate are shown in a scene "Queen of the Highway," their cage being covered by a wire screen on the side next to the audience. While fighting about the wolves broke the screen and one struggled through the opening. He sprang down among the orchestra chairs and at once the audience began a wild struggle for the exits. Somebody struck the wolf as he leaped over the chairs and he fell to the floor. As he rose he seized Mrs. Nora

Baumgarden, of 38 Guernsey Street, by the ankle. She screamed and fell unconscious.

Several women had been thrown to the floor in the first stampede. One of these was Mrs. Fannie Berhaiser, of 18 George Street, whose arms were bare. The wolf seized one of them and tore it badly. He then leaped at Mrs. Florence Johnson and bit both her arms, when a man kicked him away. A number of stagehands now formed a circle about the wolf and began to drive it back toward the stage. In a few moments several policemen forced their way into the theatre and joined the stagehands. Owing to the panic in the theatre they could not shoot.

Policeman Cosgrove leaped over several persons and landed on top of the wolf, at the same time gripping it by the throat. He threw the animal to the stage and it leaped back instantly. He seized it again and Mortch, a stagehand, caught the animal by the hind legs. Together they carried it to the stage and placed it in its cage. The manager of the theatre announced that the wolves would not again appear in the show, in spite of the panic the performance was continued after a quarter of an hour intermission.

—*Olean Evening Times*
December 21, 1910

A Favorite Place For Suicides

NEW YORK- New York mixes its contrarieties thoroughly, writes a correspondent from that city. Witness the fact that its famous playground, Central Park, is its place for tragedies. The wheels of millionaires' carriages roll on the asphalt roads past the seats of wretches desperate with hunger. The hoofs of gay equestrians' horses raise dust that settles on the rags of miserable tramps. The secluded walks and shadowed recesses are thronged in the evening by paired lovers, and in the morn- ings the bodies of suicides are found in these same sentimental retreats by the police.

Central Park has become the chosen death place of so many people that there is an average of one suicide per day there. Most of them get bare mention in the papers, but the yield of interesting matter is so large that the Police Station in the park is one of the points to which each city editor sends a reporter every midnight. The courtship of the poor of New York—especially of servants who are denied facilities for the essential sort of thing indoors—is largely done in Central Park.

The policemen drive out the coupes at 10 o'clock in the evening, and it is like shepherd dogs clearing vast flocks of sheep out of the woods. Guards are maintained at the gates during the rest of the night, but it is easy to gain entrance elsewhere over the low stone wall. The waters of the lakes offer absolutely costless means of death: the limbs of the trees require the scanty outfit of a noose for strangulation, and to those able to buy poison or with a knife to open a vein, the turf proves a soft bed for unwaking sleep. Had all the suicides been buried where they died, Central Park would have been so much a cemetery that no objection could have been made to the interment of Grant. And if the motives of all self-murderers could be learned there would need to be no further invention of themes for novels and plays.

—*Dallas Morning News*
October 5, 1885

Remarkable Rising

SYRACUSE- The remarkable freak of nature in the garden of Albert Smith at South Bodus—that of the sudden rising of a considerable area, about thirty feet square—was described in the Lyons Republican last week. It is still the subject of much discussion and wonders among the people of that locality. More than six hundred people have ridden from miles away to see the strange sight. Since last week the elevated land had risen a few inches more, but the rise has been so slow that it has been almost imperceptible.

—*Syracuse Daily Standard*
July 10, 1886

Frightening Superstitious People

ALBANY- At 10:01 last night four successive earthquake shocks were felt in this city. They were not very severe and as far as known did no damage aside from frightening superstitious people.

—*Olean Democrat*
September 2, 1886

EXTRA! EXTRA!

In 1892 Ellis Island opened in New York Harbor. It served as the primary immigration depot in the U.S.

A Seven By Thirteen Coincidence

GLEN'S FALLS- Nathaniel Witherell, who died at Glen's Falls, N.Y., always regarded himself a living oddity. He was the thirteenth child and the seventh son of his parents and the youngest child in the family. Mrs. Witherell, who still survives her husband, occupies the same relative position in her father's family, being the thirteenth and youngest child and the seventh daughter of her parents. When Mr. Witherell died they had been married sixty-five years, five times thirteen.

—*Syracuse Sunday Standard*
September 13, 1891

Helped By A Spook
Great Bend Farmer Lies Some Confidence In Spiritualism

LERAY- Leonard Blodget, a young farmer who lives near Great Bend, a few miles from this city in the town of Leray, had made up his mind since a recent mysterious experience, that as he expresses it, "there is more to spiritualism that most people think." He tells the following story to account for his recent accession of faith in the occult doctrines of the sect.

On the occasion of the recent spiritualistic mass meeting held at Washington Hall, in this city. Mr. Blodget and his wife, who were in town doing some trading, happened to wander into Washington Hall, where the meetings were held. They became interested and when Medium E. W. Sprague went into a trance and described to those who stood up for the test the appearance of the heavenly visitors who hovered near them. Blodget, in a fit of curiosity arose also. The form and features of a departed friend, who had been a fellow farm hand with him previous to his coming here from Arupior, Canada, were accurately described to him, and the first name, "Ames," correctly given, but here the medium became confused with another

person, who arose nearby, and the test ended unsatisfactory.

Blodget and his wife drove home, and upon reaching the farm, which they had leased last year, the young farmer unlocked the padlock, which fastened the house barn door, and led the horse in, securing the door in the inside with a hook. The horse barn and the kitchen of the house were connected by doors opening from each into a woodshed, the outside door of the shed being securely fastened on the inner side. While Mrs. Blodget groped her way through the dark shed to the kitchen, to get a lantern, the husband proceeded to unhitch his horse from the cutter, in the dark. He declares that "just" as he had unbuckled and tied up the holdbacks, and was unfastening the leg that side, he thought he "felt something tugging at the harness on the opposite side." At first he supposed that his wife had returned to assist him, but just at that moment he heard her voice from the vicinity of the kitchen, asking where he had left the lantern. He then stood there in the darkness, with "a kind of a creepy feeling crawling over him," as he puts it, until his wife appeared with the lighted lantern. The he took the light and cautiously edged around to the off side of the horse, but there was no one there. But the tug was unhitched, and nearly but peculiarly tied up, "just," he asserts, "as Ames would have done it," while the line and holdback strap were also unhitched and tied up.

Arming himself with a convenient pitchfork, and with his better half, who refused to remain alone, accompanying him with the lantern, Blodget avers that he searched

the barn from top to bottom, looking through stalls, granary, and hay loft. Then the couple searched the house, from cellar to garret, but, to use the farmer's own words, "Not a hide nor hair of anything could we find." He had never been able to solve the mystery surrounding his midnight assistant.

As a result of this "spookish" experience, Boldget's wife insisted on not renting the farm for another year, their lease expiring March 1st. "I told her," said he "that if we stayed somebody might come around and help me do my haying, but she allowed she didn't want that kind of help," so the haunted man will remove to another farm neat North Wilma, where he expects to be safe from spiritual manifestations.

—*Syracuse Sunday Herald*
February 27, 1898

Stone Coffin Found
Freak Of Nature Unearthed On Grindstone Island By Quarrymen

WATERTOWN- A party of local scientists went from this city to Grindstone Island, St. Lawrence River yesterday by the quarrymen of that place. They returned well placed with the result of their trip. The "freak" they described as a natural stone coffin or sarcophagus, which was unearthed by the workmen under a strain of granite four feet in thickness.

This "coffin" they found to be six and one-half feet in length, twenty-eight inches wide and twenty inches deep. The shape of the cavity is exactly that of a coffin, being wider at the point where the shoulders of an occupant would come and tapering toward the feet and head. At the foot of the cavity are well defined marks, which have the appearance of having been made by the struggling of some occupant entombed alive in what was at the time plastic material, though this is merely a matter of fancy, suggested to the party by the likeness which the cavity bears to a coffin. A report of this curious "find" has been sent to the state geologist.

—*Syracuse Herald*
March 20, 1898

"Hoodoo" Station
Fatal Accident And Disasters Follow Those Who Have Occupied It

BROOKLYN- The precinct in Brooklyn where the Atlantic police station is situated, corner of Atlantic Avenue and Schenectady Avenue, is known among policemen as the "hoodoo" precinct. The latest manifestation of the "hoodoo" influence, according to the police, is the death of Policeman John Quinn of No. 1473 Dean Street, who had a stroke of apoplexy which caused him to fall downstairs in the station house with fatal results.

The "hoodoo" has been at work in the precinct for 20 years. Its first victim was Capt. Rufus W. Crofts, who died while in command of the precinct. He was succeeded by Capt. John Riley, whose life the "hoodoo" spared, who was mixed up in so

much trouble that he was summarily dismissed from the force on June 25, 1881. William Folk, the next man in command, died on March 23, 1892.

He was succeeded by Capt. Edwin Dyer, who died in February last, after a lingering illness. Sergt. James P. White, who had been in command of a Jamaica precinct, succeeded Folk, but he was soon transferred, the present incumbent, Capt. Thomas H. Collins, then taking command. Capt. Collins is now in a precarious position at his home.

—*Syracuse Standard*
December 17, 1898

Eagle Village Boy Gets Lost In City
George Beasley Comes To Syracuse To Visit His Grandmother And Cannot Find Her

SYRACUSE- George Beasley of Eagle Village, near Manlius, 12 years old, came to this city yesterday to visit his grandmother, whom he supposed, lived in Cedar Street. The youth was unable to find the place and after a long search he appealed to a policeman to help him. The officer sent him to headquarters and at 2 o'clock George was put aboard a Suburban car and sent home.

—*Syracuse Post Standard*
May 5, 1901

Flatiron Building Declared A Nuisance

NEW YORK- An action is to be brought in the courts here to declare the eighteen-story Flatiron building a public and private nuisance. The complaint is the occupant of a store on Broadway, whose plate glass windows have been broken twice by the wind during the past three months. He holds the building responsible for the antics of the wind, the currents striking the structure and being deflected to the street and against his windows.

—*Milwaukee Journal*
January 23, 1903

The Flatiron Building was added to the National Register of Historic Places in 1979.

Dog's Leap From Bridge
Policemen Believe That It Was A Deliberate Suicide

BROOKLYN- Policemen were discussing last evening the question as to whether a dog that jumped off the Brooklyn Bridge in the afternoon committed suicide. A dozen of them in a train at 4 o'clock saw a fox terrier trot along the roadway beyond the Manhattan tower, and then leap off. A few minutes before the dog had peered at the water below.

"Looking for a place to commit suicide," one of the policemen remarked, and the passengers laughed. "By jingo, he's done it," the joking policeman said. The body was not seen afterward, although the policemen watched for it.

—*New York Times*
March 2, 1903

Beer To Be Tried
Women Bid On The Privilege Of Marrying Him

HOBOKEN- Joseph Beer, a young man living at No. 37 Clinton Street, Hoboken, will be arraigned before Justice of the Peace George F. Seymour of that city on Monday next on complaint of Matilda Toeppen, a Jewess, living in New York. Miss Toeppen says that she became acquainted with Beer through a Hebrew matrimonial agent, and Beer promised to marry her upon the payment of $200. She paid the cash, and was greatly surprised when she learned that Beer had transferred his affections to another woman, who paid him the sum of $800 for the privilege of becoming his wife. Miss Toeppen insists that Beer shall marry her, and so caused his arrest.

—*Syracuse Evening Herald*
September 15, 1899

And The Cat Came Back
Rochester Conductor Tries In Vain To Get Rid Of The Family Feline

ROCHESTER- When Rochester train, Erie Division, No. 17 pulled into the station in Court Street this afternoon, several railroad men who were standing alongside, making an inspection for members of the "hobo" tribe saw a cat perched in the truck under one of the cars. The cat was covered with dust, and showed the effects of a long hard journey. As the train came to a standstill the feline alighted and was in the act of scampering off. The conductor came along and recognized it as the family cat, which he had vainly endeavored to get rid of for a month. When the train left Rochester Conductor Walker carried the cat with him. At Corning he put the cat overboard, with the intention of losing it. The animal, however, refused to be lost, and boarding the truck of one of the cars, "dead beat" its passages back to this city.

The railroaders declared that the cat was even outdoing "Railroad Jack," the famous tramp dog that has so often ridden through here aboard trains of every class. The cat, however, preferred the hobo style of traveling.

—*New York Times*
July 13, 1900

Wanted To Lynch Italian
He Chased Boys With Stiletto. Was Knocked Down And Locked Up.

NEW YORK- Michael Agazzino, a fruit dealer of 33 East Sixty-first Street, was locked up in the East Sixty-seventh Street Station last night accused by Thomas Donoghue, a laborer of 361 East Sixty-fifth Street of trying to cut him with a stiletto. A crowd of excited men and women seized the Italian at Battle Row, Second Avenue and Sixty-first Street, and there were cries of "Lynch him," but the police protected the man.

Agazzino had been drinking the police said, and he quarreled with some boys. He was running after them with his stiletto, and had almost caught up with one of them when Donoghue hit the Italian in the face and knocked him down. He got up and tried to stab Donoghue, who eluded him, and some one knocked him down again. "Lynch him! Kill him!' were the cries that came from dozens of the men and women who quickly gathered, and some caught hold of the Italian and dragged him along the street. Bicycle Policeman Quinn, Patrolman Grey of the East Sixty-seventh Street Station and several other policemen rescued the Italian who was faint from fear, and he was half carried to the station house.

—*New York Times*
July 13, 1900

Found Two Pots Of Gold

STANTON ISLAND- Melville E. Wygant of Port Richmond, S.I., and three of his stablemen are said to have stayed up all last evening guarding a [illegible] which was found yesterday [illegible] of gold fashioned chimney when an old Hatfield [illegible] was torn down on the Wygant homestead. Yesterday, while Wygant's men were removing bricks from the chimney, they came upon two copper kettles, in which they found, to their astonishment, gold bullion, and coin in $5, $10, and $20 denominations. The latest date on any of the coins was 1866.

There are many rumors as to the value of the gold, some reports placing it in the thousands. Mr. Wygant is silent on the subject, declaring first to find out whose

the treasure legally is. It is said that he buried the kettles and their rich contents in the stable, and then, with three of his men, mounted guard on the building for the night.

—*Syracuse Post Standard*
May 31, 1901

Methodist Elm Accused Of Graft
More Likely A Case Of Unusual Attachment

CLYDE- A freak of nature has been discovered in the yard of the M. E. Church parsonage, where the branch of an elm tree has grown away from the parent trunk, and them made a turn and grown right back into the same trunk again. The second union with the trunk is probably a natural growth.

—*Syracuse Post Standard*
September 7, 1904

The "13" Hoodoo Has Gone
Polhemus Place, Brooklyn, Can Get Servants Now.

BROOKLYN- The Street Numbering Bureau of Brooklyn told Henry B. Plumb of 13 Polhemus Place yesterday that he could scratch the hoodoo off his front door. It gave him a neat slip of paper authorizing him the name of the Borough of Brooklyn to substitute a numerical mascot. He was told that under the powers of the permit he could hang the left hind foot of a rabbit caught in a graveyard at midnight, under the new number in case the hoodoo proved stubborn.

Maybe Mr. Plumb can get a servant now. Mrs. Plumb is hopeful, and there is an air of optimism and cheerfulness about the family in marked comparison to the gloom and depression of those bitter days when Bridget and Mary Ann and black Hannah and tow-headed Gretchen shuffled into the tiny street and up to the Plumb door and then turned away again, noses in the air. The whole neighborhood has taken on a brighter look.

Polhemus Place is a little thumbnail, one block thoroughfare, connecting Carroll Street with Garfield Place. It is as prim as an old maid. Save for the clatter of trolley cars on Seventh Avenue, it is as quiet as a church. It is a sort of Millionaire's Row and servants are well paid, but butlers and housemaids and scullions and coachmen avoided it as they would have dodged a plague spot. It is hard to get servants anyway in Brooklyn, it is said, but in Polhemus Place it was well-nigh impossible.

The gilt 13 in the front door of the Plumb house was the cause of the trouble. It not only scared domestics away from the Plumbs, but it seemed to hoodoo the whole neighborhood. The reason was that Mr. Plumb's house is the first on the left hand side from Carroll Street, and servants catching a glimpse of the wretched 13, scurried away from the neighborhood. That has been going on for years. Mr.

Plumb, who is the secretary of a concern at 105 Chambers Street, Manhattan, has been spending lots of money advertising for servants. His advertisements drew hundreds of domestics to the door, but that was all. He couldn't get them inside. One look at the grim 13 drove them away in a hurry. Argument, entreaty, offers of double wages, didn't do a bit of good. There wasn't one of them that was willing to take chances with fate by working in a house with a 13 on its front door.

The nationality of the domestics didn't seem to make a bit of difference. Irish cooks, German housemaids, English coachmen, negro kitchen help, it was all the same. The baleful 13 sent them scurrying. Finally Mr. Plumb made up his mind that the only way to end the intolerable situation was to change the house number. Yesterday he want to the Bureau of Complaints and asked Supervisor James A. Rooney how the number could be changed. He was rather averse to giving a reason for the unusual request until the Supervisor informed him that under the rules the reason had to be set forth to the Street Numbering Bureau.

"I'm not superstitious and I don't take any stock in all this nonsense about the number 13, but it's a matter of dollars and cent and I've got to have it changed, that's all there is about it," he said. "Possibly your wife is superstitious," suggested Rooney. "Not at all," replied Mr. Plumb. "She doesn't lose a bit of sleep because she is on a house numbered 13. She would be willing to move on Friday and I have some reason to believe that she would walk under a ladder without a tremor. I am positive she could spill salt without being horrified, and there is no doubt in the world that black cats are of no especial significance to her any more than they are to me."

"Well, what in the world---------" began the Supervisor of the grumble board. "Why, it's simply that we can't get servants as long as that blamed number stares applicants in the face when they come to look for a job. You've no idea how the cost of advertising in the daily papers for house help mounts up. It's a case of spending money for advertising every day and getting no results at all, because you are unlucky enough to live where the door of your house bears a 1 and a 3. The thing got to such a pass after a time that we did not put the number of the house into the ads, knowing that would be plain foolishness. We thought that we would have a chance with our persuasive powers after the applicants got to the house. But it wasn't a bit of use. They came in droves, but they departed in haste."

Rooney sympathized and looked up the plot of the street to see what could be done. He found that a vacant lot next to Mr. Plumb's house had been bought up by people living on Carroll Street for the purpose of deepening their backyards. Consequently the vacant lot ceased to have the existence as a part of Polhemus Place, and the number it would have borne became available for Mr. Plumb's use. Hereafter the Plumb house will be No. 11 and the house adjoining on the other side will be No. 15.

Mr. Plumb says that nothing ever happened in the house to give added color to

the 13 superstition. He has lived there a good many years, he says, and he can't remember a single accident or misfortune that could be attributed, even by the biggest stretch of imagination, to the malevolent influence of the number 13.

—*Dallas Morning News*
May 14, 1905

The fear of the number 13 is called Triskaidekaphobia.

Woman's Curiosity Unveils Tombstones
Four Shafts That Once Marked Graves Used As A Sidewalk By Solvay People

SOLVAY- Chiseled and cut with care, four tombstones which once marked the graves of as many members of the Steves family, serve as a sidewalk in the yard of a Solvay house occupied by the family of Michael E. Casey.

Until yesterday afternoon no one knew the real nature of the stones. Curiosity got the best of Mrs. Casey and she resolved to have them overturned. This done, the following inscriptions were brought to light: Rev. John W. Steves, died July 17, 1860, aged 62 years, 2 months, and 12 days. Hannah, wife of J. Bunker and daughter of Rev. John W. Steves, died January 18, 1858, aged 32 years. Jeremiah, son of Rev. John W. Steves, died September 8, 1857, aged 27 years. George Gary Steves, died February 5, 1847, aged 21 years, 3 months and 23 days.

The Steves family lived in the Nockett as a tract of land west of the lake is called, and in the old North Church Elder Steves held forth to his little congregation and taught the way to the higher life. The cemetery which the stones once graced was broken up years ago. The stones come into the possession of J. D. Grover of Solvay, who built the house at No. 403 Second Street, and he used them as a sidewalk.

—*Syracuse Post Standard*
August 7, 1905

EXTRA! EXTRA!

On October 28, 1886, the Statue of Liberty was dedicated in New York Harbor.

Broken-Hearted Parrot
Dave Kraushaar, City Marshal, Vouches For This Tale.

NEW YORK- "Dewey," a Mexican parrot, the pride of City Marshal David Krausharr of 460 Grand Street, is in the ice box waiting for such immortality as a taxidermist can give him. He could yell louder than all the peddlers of the east side and swear as skillfully as any Delancey Street patrolman.

No envious neighbor, no sleepless victim did Dewey to death. It was lack of nourishment, and incidentally, Marshal Kraushaar says, a broken heart that brought about his end. He had the skill to sing to the air of "The Star Spangled Banner" the famous old lines "Oh, Dewey was the morning," and this alone had long protected him from the violence of other families in the apartment houses.

Since the Marshal bought the bird in Mexico at the time of the war with Spain the chief admirer and devoted caretaker of Dewey had been Mrs. Kraushaar. Seven weeks ago she went away for a summer vacation, and left the bird in charge of her husband. He fed and cared for it to the best of his ability, but it languished and didn't eat. The marshal says Dewey would plaintively call over and over again: "Mamma, oh Mamma!" which was its way of calling Mrs. Kraushaar. She returned last evening. The bird had its head under its wing. It was on the bottom of the cage, too weak to stand on the perch. Mrs. Kraushaar spoke to her pet, calling him by name. He lifted his head, opened an eye, said "Oh Mamma," tried to get up, sang as far as "Oh, Dewey was the morning," and fell back dead. It was too late to find a taxidermist last night, and that's why Dewey was placed in the icebox.

—New York Times
September 7, 1906

Battle With Tiger Cub
Beast Attacked Miss Beet.
Her Father Kills It.

BENSONHURST- Thomas Beet, proprietor of a private detective agency, who lives at 172 Bay Thirty-fourth Street, Bensonhurst, had a fierce battle yesterday with a tiger cub, which had been a pet in his home and had the freedom of the house like a dog or cat. The struggle occurred when the beast suddenly became ferocious and turned on Mr. Beet's six-year old daughter Dorothy.

Mr. Beet finally killed the cub by asphyxiating it in a gas oven, but the encounter left him weak from fright over his daughter's narrow escape. Empress, as Mr. Beet's children, Dorothy and Mildred called the beast, was the gift of Capt. Cyrus Welden, skipper of a craft in the South American trade. Capt. Weldon caught the cub when it was only two months old and gave it to Mr. Beet several months ago. Empress played with the Beet children like a big cat. It had always seemed to be gentle and Mr. and Mrs. Beet felt no hesitancy in letting their little ones make a pet of it. Recently however, Empress had become sulky and restive, and Mr. Beet was thinking her to a zoo. Still he did not chain the

beast up, although he warned the children against playing too roughly with it.

Yesterday Mr. Beet was sitting in his parlor, when he heard his daughter Dorothy screaming in the kitchen. Thinking immediately of Empress, Mr. Beets ran into the room and found Dorothy cowering in the corner. Before the girl crouched Empress, her lips drawn back over her fangs and her tail swinging, while she snarled menacingly. Mr. Beet was unarmed, but as the beast seemed about to spring upon the girl he sprang forward, and kicked it in the head. The blow knocked Empress over, but she was on her feet like a flash, crouched and lashing her tail in fury.

Again Mr. Beet kicked Empress and as she toppled over he kept up his attack shouting to Dorothy to run. The girl obeyed and as the cub staggered to her feet still bent on fight, Mr. Beet thought of the gas range and swung open the over door. Then he caught up Empress despite her snarls and scratching and whipped her into the oven, slammed the door shut, and turned in the gas. For five minutes Mr. Beet held the oven door while Empress thrashed about inside. At last, however, her struggles ceased, and when Mr. Beet opened the door the cub was dead.

—New York Times
January 11, 1908

Mad Bull In Street

**Batted Into State Street Entrance
Of Court House.
Was Killed By O. R. Casey.
Farmers Had Heard
On Way To Slaughter House
When Bull Became Mad
And Fought To Get Away.
Dragged Men In Road.**

SYRACUSE- A snorting angry bull, charging through the streets in the vicinity of the Court House, with two men tugging on ropes about the animal's neck to prevent him from doing possible harm to pedestrians or properly, was the spectacle witnessed by hundreds of people in the neighborhood between 1 and 1:30 o'clock this afternoon.

The mad flight of the animal ended in his being put to death by O. R. Casey of the Society for the Prevention of Cruelty to Animals, after the animal had made an infectious attempt to bust his way into the Court House and after he had been securely tied to a big tree at the corner of Montgomery and Madison Streets. The bull was one of a herd of nine cattle being taken to Hoffman's slaughter house in Free Street by Philip Fredman of Fabina. Two men started with the herd, which consisted of six cows and three bulls. There was no trouble on the way in from the country. After reaching the city the bull which afterward caused the trouble was noticed by the two men in charge to grow restless.

Just before Jefferson Street was reached in State Street the animal broke from the heard and started toward the Court House. He lowered his head and butted with all his might against the doors of the South State Street entrance. The men held tight to the ropes and succeeded in diverting the course of the animal. The doors of the Court House shook and the bull turned about and started down the street. He turned into Cedar Street, the men pulling vigorously on the ropes and crying to people to get out of the way. Every one within a block of the animal darted for a piece of safety. Reaching Montgomery Street the bull turned to the south, tugging to get away and the men clinging desperately at the ropes to hold him. He dragged them to the corner of Madison Street when one of the men succeeded in getting his end of the rope about a hydrant. He snubbed the bovine in good shape and the other man got his end of the rope around about the trunk of a tree. Then they wound the ropes around the bull's neck several times and made a safe knot about the tree.

The men were exhausted from their efforts. One of them went to a telephone after he had taken a rest and called up Mr. Casey. When Casey arrived he put two balls from a 38-caliber revolver into the animal's brain. The bull made one mighty attempt to get to his feet after the first shot and there was a wild scramble among the several hundred people which had gathered to get out of the way. At the second shot the bull quivered, fell on his haunches and then rolled over dead.

—*Syracuse Herald*
October 2, 1907

Curious Coincidence
Mr. Barnett's Brother-in-law
Bound For The Bench

MIDDLETOWN- Harry B. Davis, a
brother-in-law of Leo Barnett, of this city,
has been nominated by the Independence
League of the 6th district of Manhattan for
the city judge and his nominations has
been endorsed by the Republicans. A curious coincidence is that another brother-in-
law of Mr. Barnett, ex-Senator Jacob
Marks has been nominated also for the
same office, in the same district by
Tammany.
—Middletown Orange County Times
October 15, 1907

Policeman Knocked Off
Brooklyn Bridge
Chasing A Maniac
Who Wanted To Jump
And A Passing Trolley Car Hit Him.
Fight Among The Girders.
Would-be Suicide Almost Throws
Two More Patrolmen.
Finally Knocked Senseless
And Carried Away.

BROOKLYN- "There's a crazy man trying to jump off the bridge down below!"
shouted a man on the Brooklyn Bridge
walk to Policeman Robert J. Fitzgerald of
the Bridge Squad at 11:30 o'clock last
night.

Some distance from him and near the
Manhattan anchorage tower Fitzgerald
saw a man clambering down one of the
ladders that leads from the walk to the
tracks used by the elevated trains below.
The policemen followed in the run. The
man ahead reached the elevated tracks and
darted out on the roadway alongside the
tracks, squeezing through the filigree of
iron work that separates the elevated from
the trolley tracks on the bridge roadway.

Fitzgerald saw the man start toward the
guard rail at the side of the roadway and he
sprang down the ladder and tried to
squeeze through the trestle work on to the
roadway. So intent was he on the chase
that he did not see a trolley car flying along
the tracks. It was a Putnam Avenue car
bound for New York and Motorman
Edward Conlon was at the controller. He
saw the policeman just as the latter saw the
car. It was too late for either to do any-

thing. The front of the car hit the policeman. He screamed. His body was forced back through the trestle, and he dropped between the ties into the river below. The man on the roadway had stopped to watch.

Conlon stopped his car, and Policeman Scannell and Sergt. Farrell ran up. They saw the man whom Fitzgerald had been chasing, just as he climbed back through the trestle on to the railroad tracks. Scannell followed him, while Farrell ordered Conlon to hasten to Manhattan and start a search for Fitzgerald's body. Scannell overtook his man and grappled with him. The man showed exceptional strength and tried to throw the policeman off the bridge. Together they struggled for several minutes, narrowly escaping the third rail, which is not covered or protected, and in momentary danger of falling between the ties into the river below.

At last Farrell climbed through the trestle and went to Scannell's aid. Even then the policeman could not subdue then man. He fought them both, and it seemed that he would accomplish his purpose of throwing himself or them into the water. A few blows from Farrell's nightstick at last subdued him, leaving him nearly senseless, and then the two policemen carried him to a car and started for the Bridge Station in Brooklyn. There the man at first declined to give his name. It was apparent that he was demented. He appeared to be about 20 years old, and was stockily built. He said he had no home, and would tell no more about himself. Then he admitted that he was Edward H. Walker of Wabash Avenue, Chicago. In his pockets were found a Pennsylvania Railroad pass

between Cresson and Spangler and two transfers of the Chicago Union Traction Company, neither of the latter bearing a date, and a ticket to a Chicago skating rink. A seal ring the man were bore the initials "E.H.W." He had no money except a small Spanish copper coin. The harbor police started a search for Fitzgerald's body, but early this morning it was unsuccessful.

—*New York Times*
January 11, 1908

A Strange Coincidence
Brothers Meeting After Two Years Find Each Has Lost Hand

SYRACUSE- When Edward Burgman of Milwaukee arrived in this city yesterday to visit his brother Charles, whom he had not seen for two years, he learned for the first time that Charles had lost his hand. Charles in turn discovered that Edward too had a hand amputated since their meeting.

Charles, who was formerly a baker lives at No. 311 West Division Street. He lost his hand in an accident with a baking machine which made necessary the amputation of his right arm near the shoulder. Edward had his left arm cut off in a flouring mill in the West.

—*Syracuse Herald*
January 16, 1908

Would Reward The Thief
May Have Valuables If He Will Return Mrs. Morton's Keepsakes

NEW YORK- Mrs. Howard Morton, prominent in society and D.A.R. circles of New York and Greenwich, whose jewels were stolen while she and her father were at dinner, has appealed to the sympathies of the thief through an advertisement in which she offers to negotiate for the return of her jewels, giving more for them in cash than any pawnbroker would offer.

"Twenty-eight articles of jewelry were taken," said Mrs. Morton, "and while I do not know just what their value is, I value them much more than their intrinsic worth. For instance, there was my diamond solitaire engagement ring, a good serpent bracelet with engraving thereon, a blue enamel pin, a gift of a dear friend, and an oval pin set with a green stone which came from a particular friend of mine and was unique, and a pendent with it; also a pink

topaz necklace. The diamond sunburst was worth more than all the rest together, but I would gladly let the thief keep it if he would give me back the trinkets I most prize."

—Syracuse Herald
January 22, 1908

Thieves Worked; Police Ate
Patrolman Lunched On Steps Of E. D. Page's Home. Burglars Tried To Get In.

NEW YORK- While two policemen were sitting on the front steps of the residence of Edward D. Page at 238 East Fifteenth Street eating a lunch early last Tuesday morning burglars attempted to enter the house.

A governess of the family heard them and her screams frightened them away. The police suppressed the report of the attempted robbery, but Mrs. Page told of it last night. The burglars descended from the roof of the Page residence by the fire escape and began to force an entrance through one of the rear windows. A governess was awakened by the noise and ran to the front window and screamed. Two patrolmen of the East Twenty-second Street Station were seated on the steps of the Page house eating their lunch, according to members of the Page family. Mr. Page then searched the premises but the burglars had escaped.

—New York Times
March 17, 1908

EXTRA! EXTRA!

The first Boy's Club was established in New York City in 1876.

Sues For His "Spirit" Home
Lawyer White Says Spook Medium Got Him To Buy It For Here

LONG ISLAND- Believing that a message he received in July, 1902, from his dead wife was a sham, David S. White, a Manhattan lawyer, has instituted legal proceedings in Suffolk County, L.I., to gain possession to the title to some property he purchased for her at his dead wife's spirit's behest. White married Margaret Gaylord and they lived in Hoboken, until the wife's death on May 13, 1901. In the summer following her death he met the spirit medium, Henrietta L. Woodhouse. The defendant stated to him that she would communicate with his wife or her spirit, so that he might learn her wishes.

He received an alleged message from his wife that it was her wish that he should purchase a place in the country, out on Long Island, and have the title in the medium's name. He purchased the home of Phebe J. Overton, and had the deed made in the name of the defendant. The medium immediately took possession of the "soul-message" place and has since occupied it, notwithstanding his recent demands that she vacate the premises, and turn over to him the title now vested in her.

—*New York Times*
May 13, 1908

Made A Floating Island
Large Section Of Land Broke Away From Shore Of Lake Neahtawanta

FULTON- A freak of nature was observed from the shores of Lake Neahtawanta this morning when it became apparent that a considerable island had suddenly made its appearance in the middle of the lake. But the observers who noticed the freak at first were nonplussed, when a few moments later as they glanced out towards the island to find that its location had changed and that it was much nearer the eastern shore of the lake then the first seen. Observation disclosed the fact that the new island was moving slowly and majestically towards the fair grounds shore where it touched and became anchored about 10 o'clock this morning.

Investigation proved that a portion of land about three-quarters of an acre in extent had broken loose from the lake shore near North Bay and carried by the wind and current had wended its way for a mile and a quarter southeastward through the lake.

Trees of considerable size and number remained in their upright position during the transit and seem as soundly rooted as their kind on that portion of terra firma which has not shown migratory tendencies.

—*Syracuse Herald*
June 21, 1908

Friday Hoodoo Lands On Johnny Once More
Fifth Day's Proverbial Misfortune Comes When He Is Hurt For Fourth Time

SYRACUSE- Unlucky Johnny Davidson of No. 225 West Kennedy Street dodged his Friday hoodoo for two years, but it came back last night. Four times he has been injured off the fifth day of the week.

As he was on his way downtown to see the parade with his uncle the uncle gave him a penny to spend. He started to run across Cortland Avenue and was struck by a Rapid Transit car. When picked up it was found that he had sprained his wrist and Dr. H. O. Brust was called to attend him. Next year he is going to request that the Mystique Krewe select another night than Friday for the school children's parade. Johnny was 9 years old on June 25. His most serious accident was on February 9, 1904, when he fell down stairs and fractured his skull. January 29, 1904, he plunged into Onondaga Creek while coasting and one week later was chewed by a vicious bulldog.

—*Syracuse Post Standard*
September 19, 1908

Finds Freak In Garden That Baffles Botanists

SYRACUSE- Frederick Haynes of No. 217 Hoyden Street yesterday dug from his garden specimens that botanical students could not identify. One of the freaks is to be sent to Cornell University scientists for their examination. Mr. Hayes was attracted to a portion of his garden yesterday morning by several small objects a few inches above ground. They were similar in color to cocoons, cigar shaped. Mr. Hayes carefully unearthed several small sacs or eggs, which were connected with a small thread of the same substance.

Mr. Haynes laid his find on the furnace. From one of the eggs came a long orange-colored core which later almost withered away, turning red. With the others in a tin box, Mr. Haynes came to the Post-Standard office, but when he opened the box he was surprised to find another core in the box, which had matured on the way. Half its length was bright orange in color, while the end was a deep green. The object was very fragile. Mr. Haynes showed the specimens to several florists, none of whom were able to tell what they were. Some expressed the thought they belonged to the mushroom family.

—*Syracuse Post Standard*
January 5, 1909

A Strange Funeral
No Flowers, No Prayers Said, No Hymns Sung.
Only Old Cronies Of Brother Of Syracuse Women Gathered And They Did Not Mourn, But Told Stories Of Man's Whimsicalities.

NEW YORK- One of the strangest funerals ever held in New York was that of Col. John M. Otter a brother of Mrs. Ann Eliza Ellerton of this city, which took place from the home of the deceased late last evening.

No prayer was said, no hymns were sung, there was not a clergyman present or a flower upon the coffin of the aged man, who once handled all the T. Stewart Hotel interests in New York and Saratoga. In the will of the deceased were left directions for the strange funeral service which was not properly speaking a service at all, but merely a farewell session of fifteen or so of old cronies of Colonel Otter's "House of Lords."

The fifteen men, none of whom is under 65, and some of whom are more than 80 years old, sat around the plain mahogany coffin in the parlor and told stories of their dead friend's whimsicalities, his cheery optimism and unfailing good humor. That was all of the service. To-day the body was buried in Greenwood.

Colonel Otter was a man who believed that after death there was nothing more. He had always said that the lamentations and forms of grief attending the stereotyped funerals revolted him and he did not wish that even a flower should be deprived of life in order to wither on his coffin.

Colonel Otter established his "House of Lords" in 1899. He was then 75 years old, but he insisted that no man was grown up until he was at least 65. He made the prime requisite of membership the possession of at least that number of years.

One of Colonel Otter's sisters, Mrs. Rebecca Chase of New York, was buried at the very hour her brother died on Tuesday. Mrs. Ellerton, who is 91 years old, was unable, on account of her advanced years, to be present at her brother's funeral. She makes her home with relative in this city. Another sister, Mrs. William Thorn, live in Jersey City.

—*Syracuse Herald*
March 5, 1909

Hoodoo On Household
Jacob Freiburg's Accident Completes Chain.
Bicycle Weekend.

SYRACUSE- When Jacob Freiburg of No. 1019 West Onondaga street, an employee of the National Chemical Company, was struck by an automobile and knocked from his bicycle at Jefferson and South Salina Streets that evening, an unusual string of accidents was completed, every member of the household having been injured in some way with the past few weeks.

Freiburg, who lives with S. G. Brown, the manager of the company, was detained in the office with another clerk until 10:30 o'clock last night with Mr. Brown. At that hour they started home, Mr. Brown taking the car and the boys riding their bicycles. As they neared Jefferson Hotel Freiburg heard an approaching automobile and turned toward the curbstone. The automobile also made the turn toward the curb and Freiburg, seeing this, turned into East Jefferson Street. He had only gotten as far as the car track however, when the machine struck the rear wheel of his bicycle, threw him to the pavement and completely wrecked his bicycle. The chauffeur, it is said, did not stop his machine, but Freiburg stated that he had secured the last four figures of the cars registered numbers and is endeavoring to find the owner. He was not badly injured.

—*Syracuse Herald*
May 21, 1909

2 ½ Years For A Cent
John Curran,
Sentenced In Brooklyn,
Took Victim's Last Penny.

BROOKLYN- For stealing one cent John Curran was sentenced yesterday to State's prison for two and a half years by Judge Dike in the County Court Brooklyn. Thomas Quayle, the owner of the penny was standing in the doorway of a Fulton Street lodging house when Curran came along and robbed him of the coin. It was the last cent he had in the world he said.

—*New York Times*
June 15, 1909

"I Love My Sweetheart, But-"
Young Girl Takes Her Fiancé
Before Magistrate
For Talking Rudely To Dad

NEW YORK- Cella Barshak, aged 20, appeared in Essex Market court against her sweetheart, Jacob Bennett of No. 99 Fourth Street, whom she charged with abusing her father.

"I love my sweetheart, but I love my father, too," Miss Barshak told Magistrate Cornell. She said Bennett called at her house, No. 306 Broome Street, Saturday night and quarreled with her father, and when she remonstrated he threatened to strike her. "He has been keeping company with me for two years, and we hope to be married," she replied proudly. "He is a splendid young man, works hard all the time, and I'm very sorry this had occurred."

"What do you want me to do with him?" "Nothing Judge, please, except to ask him to let my father alone." "It's all the fault of her father," said Bennett. "I've never missed a night in calling on Miss Barshak for two years, and I even give her all my salary to put in the bank each week. Her father, however, drinks and won't work, and I got tired of it and called him to account last night." "I'll let you go with a reprimand," said the Magistrate. "You young people must not spoil your lives by bothering about the father." They thanked the Magistrate and departed hand in hand.

—*Syracuse Herald*
August 8, 1909

Dish-Wiper
An Opera Star
Hammerstein Finds Prize
In A Long Island Restaurant

LONG ISLAND- From dish-wiping to the stage of the Manhattan Opera House is the quick jump of the newest discovery of Oscar Hammerstein, who will introduce Antonio Richards to the New York public as additional tenor the coming winter.

The discovery was made by patrons of a fashionable restaurant in Huntington, L.I., when the American Institute of Architects dining there heard exquisite renditions of tenor parts from "Martha" and "Tosca" emanating from the pantry. They clamored for the man who, clad in his pantry-man's costume, was brought into the dining room to sing. His operatic selections made a tremendous hit. John G. Petit, designer of the stage settings, was so impressed that he declared he would introduce the singer to Mr. Hammerstein. Opportunity this opened the door for Richards to appear at the Manhattan Opera House.

Before coming to this country Richards, a fine-looking Italian, sang tenor parts in grand opera in Havana. On his arrival here necessity made him forsake his musical vocation for the lowlier calling of wiping-dishes. He has left the restaurant to prepare for the coming season, and is jubilant over his return to the operatic world.

—*Syracuse Herald*
September 19, 1909

Cat Full Of Jewels
New York Woman Seeks Pussie
Who Ran Off With $3,000 Worth

NEW YORK- If you see a cat full of diamonds and rubies and earrings and such like bawbees, run quickly and tell Mrs. Lillie Stumpf at No. 202 West Ninety-second Street. Mrs. Stumpf don't care a rap for pussy; the finder may have her when she has been thoroughly searched and she will pay $100 for the privilege of searching.

The lost gems were in a gray pocketbook, which Sadie, Mrs. Stumpf's cat, naturally mistook for a new kind of legless mouse. Willie Stumpf saw Sadie's prize and essayed to replevin it, but Sadie took to her feline heels o'er fence tops, and Willie saw her making a meal of it in the distance. The pocketbook contained a crescent brooch, containing twenty-six diamonds, a pair of diamond earrings and a ring set with sapphires, rubies and diamonds. All are worth $3,000.

—*Syracuse Herald*
October 31, 1909

Queer Proof Of Love
Girl Will Wed Man
Who Threw Acid In Her Face

NEW YORK- "Now at last I know he loves me. Now I will marry him as soon as he is free—if he wishes." Dora Steinmesser said it this afternoon. Dora used to work on flowers, but she won't make any more pink carnations or yellow roses for a good many weeks—may be never again. Night before last as she was keeping tryst with him in Stuyvesant park her lover, George Alberts, burned all her beauty and perhaps her sight, quite away. He pleaded for a kiss. When she hesitated he wrenched off her veil and dashed carbolic acid over her face and neck and even in her dark eyes. "Now no one else shall kiss you!" he muttered. "You are mine—mine—but oh, I didn't think—I'd hurt you so!"

"My face was all on fire whenever you see these," the girl said to-day pointing to the thick white bandages which almost cover her face up from forehead to throat. "It hurt me so! I couldn't help crying. But then I listened to George—for he was saying I didn't think it would be so bad—I didn't mean to kill you—and now they'll kill me and we can't be happy any more.

Don't you see he was thinking of me as well as himself? Do you suppose I could have people punish him after that?"

"For two years now I have known him. I love him. But—you see, I was not quite sure, after all, if he loved me so much. Now do you see he has proved it—he has put his mark on me, and I tell you I love him for it. Never will I look at anyone else—never, never. I am not angry with him; I will not have him punished. And no matter how I look, he will love me. We will have our wedding the day those officers let him go."

—*Syracuse Herald*
October 31, 1909

Town In Dread Of Rabies
Dog Thought To Be Mad Bites A
Man And Twenty Dogs

WHITE PLAINS- The residents of Bronxville and Bronx Manor were much excited to-day when a French bulldog owned by George W. Kneeling, a prominent citizen, supposed to be suffering from rabies, bit Mr. Kneeling and at least twenty dogs.

The dog attacked Mr. Kneeling, and before he could protest himself had fastened his teeth in the man's finger. The dog then attacked and bit six fox terrier puppies, and also bit their mother. She had to be chloroformed. The dog bit some twelve other dogs in the neighborhood before it was found dead in Lawrence Park by Policeman Taxter. Mr. Kneeling is now undergoing treatment in the Pasteur Institute in New York. Among the dogs attacked were those belonging to Supt. Flynn of Palmer Avenue, William Gray, J. McGrath, and William Leggett, all prominent residents of Bronxville. Three of the dogs were killed, but it is feared the rabies may be spread.

—*New York Times*
November 12, 1909

Fight For Suicide Rope
East Side Women Believe It Will Keep Bad Luck Away

NEW YORK- A dozen women struggling to obtain a piece of the rope which a woman neighbor had just handed herself on the roof of the five story tenement at No. 193 East Third Street, were seen by Policeman Wright when he was summoned to the roof by one of the women who had her amulet—a piece of the rope—clutched in her hand.

Wright had just turned into East Third Street when a woman rushed up to him and said: "For God's sake, go to the roof of 193. A woman has committed suicide there." Wright sped up the steps and on the roof was stretched a woman whom the others said was Mrs. Barbara Yftzan, a widow, who had lived in the house two weeks. There was only a wisp of the rope with which the woman had hanged herself left about her neck. Each woman standing around had cut as much of the rope away as she could, saying that it would serve to keep bad luck away from their household.

Mrs. Yftzan had been in bad health for some weeks and to add to her uneasiness of mind, her son, Stephen, announced to her that he intended to marry this week. The widow brooded over this and when the neighbors suggested that she go to a hospital she replied that she would rather kill herself. The suicide left this message, written on a scrap of wrapping paper: "If he thinks more of getting married than he does of me, let him go ahead, but he will have cause to regret it."

—*Syracuse Herald*
November 21, 1909

Married In A Taxicab
Convalescent Patient In New York Hospital The Bridegroom

NEW YORK- C. H. Smith, a convalescent patient at Bellevue Hospital, and Mrs. L. R. Retzell were married in a taxicab in the courtyard of the hospital, while witnesses and the officiating clergymen were all crowded in and about the vehicle. Bridesmaids alone were missing.

The odd ceremony was made necessary when Smith collapsed in the cab after a trip to the City Hall for a marriage license. Despite his weakened condition it was decided to perform the ceremony with bride and groom seated in the vehicle. The honeymoon trip consisted of a journey from the hospital to his home, with his wife acting as nurse.

—*The Syracuse Herald*
January 2, 1910

Thirteen In A Boat; Hoodoo Proves Deadly

HASTINGS- From the great mass of black clouds which swept across the Hudson River this afternoon, a bolt of lightning struck a boating party of thirteen near Hastings, killing one and severely burning two others.

The dead youth was Charles Herbert, an insurance clerk, living at No. 130 Leroy Street in this city. Beside him when the lightning felled him were William Mitty and John Drout. All three were standing close together sheltering themselves as best they could from the downpour of rain by a piece of canvas, which they pulled lightly over their heads. With an unaccountable freakishness the electricity singled out this little group from all the rest. It did absolutely no harm to the boat.

—*Syracuse Post Standard*
May 31, 1910

Bathers At Coney Island Must Don More Clothes

NEW YORK- No more one piece bathing suits for men at Coney Island and no more women in Bloomers without skirts; likewise no more stockingless of the fair young bather. Police Captain Galvain laid down the law to-day. "Personally it makes no difference to me," said the captain, "as to how the women bathers dress. Personally I don't care if they all hunt up Mother Eve's dressmaker and get a suit patterned after the first gown ever worn,

but as a police captain it is different. I think the proper costume for a woman is a three-piece suit, waist skirt and bloomers and stockings. Men must wear a two-piece suit with a reasonable length coat piece and trunks too short." As a result of the cry that has gone up against immodest bathing suits at the Island, eight men were arrested to-day.

—*Syracuse Post Standard*
August 8, 1910

In an ironic twist, Coney Island is now widely known for its bizarre sideshow performances and unique characters.

EXTRA! EXTRA!

Hartsdale established the first pet cemetery in 1896, and contains over 70,000 animals.

An Apple In Full Bloom

CORNING- Albert Waber, of Ferris Street, this city, has a freak of nature in an apple tree which is now in full bloom after having borne a crop of apples this year. Local wiseacres are at a loss to explain the phenomena of this antic on the part of the tree.

—Olean Evening Times
September 14, 1910

Names Are The Same And Men Look Alike

L. A. Wegman, Sr. and L. A. Wegman, Jr. meet at Yates. Can trace no relationship.

SYRACUSE- "L. A. Wegman, Sr." "L. A. Wegman, Jr." These two names were the cause of a strange incident at the Yates yesterday. Wegman, Sr., registered early in the morning and about 6 o'clock in the afternoon Wegman, Jr., arrived. When the latter had registered, the clerk, Larry White, thought he saw a remarkable resemblance between the two men. "Your father is in town, he registered this morning," said Mr. White. Wegman Jr., looked puzzled.

"Why," he replied, "my father has been dead since 1894. It must be his ghost." L. A Wegman, Jr., insisted he had no male relative in the world, and the last one he ever heard of was named John Wegman. Every characteristic Mr. Wegman, Jr., admitted, was true of his father. Finally it was decided to settle the matter by bringing the men together. There was indeed a striking resemblance between the two. Both were the same height, about the same weight, and their eyes of the same color. The only difference was the iron gray hair of the older and the coal black of the latter.

After a conversation of fifteen minutes they came to the conclusion that they were in no way related. "But," continued Wegman, Jr., "Are you the fellow who got all the letters from my girl when we were at the same hotel in Chicago?" Wegman, Sr., chuckled, "Why," he answered, "I thought that was only a signal from my wife that Christmas was nigh."

—Syracuse Post Standard
December 27, 1910

Undresses In Church
An Insane Printer Thinks He's In The Garden Of Eden

NEW YORK- An insane printer, who gave his name as John McDonald, created a sensation in the Roman Catholic Church of Epiphany this morning. While services were being conducted the man entered, and walking down the center aisle proceeded to remove all his clothing. An officer of the church after considerable difficulty succeeded in overpowering and ejecting McDonald, but not until many women in the audience had been badly frightened and the services interrupted.

—*Dallas Morning News*
February 18, 1894

CHAPTER 6 PECULIAR PEOPLE

Ate A Quart
Of Grasshoppers
Old Levi Layman, Of Beechwoods, Enjoys A Novel Feast.

BEECHWOODS- Levi Layman, of the Beechwoods district, who gained notoriety some time ago by announcing that his death would occur upon a certain date, long since passed, foretold to him in a dream, is attracting the attention of his neighbors by eating grasshoppers. The old man is failing very fast in health and strength and says he never has any appetite.

He says he doesn't eat as much as a child two years old. A few years ago he weighed 150 pounds and now he weighs 115 pounds. The other day he told his nearest neighbor that he had a good mess of grasshoppers he thought he could eat them. He declared that they were better than any kind of meat or fish, but said he was too old to catch them any more.

As the grasshopper crop is a particularly abundant one, this year, the neighbor willingly went out in a nearby field and captured the old gentleman a quart of the insects. These Mr. Lyman promptly fried and ate for supper, his neighbor remaining until the last "pest" had disappeared. The old man says that he believes if he had a few quarts of grasshoppers daily he could eat them and soon build up in health again.

—*Middletown Daily Argus*
July 19, 1895

John J. McKnight's Curious Will
He Wanted A Box For A Coffin And An Express Wagon For A Hearse

WHITE PLAINS- The filing of the will of John J. McKnight in the Surrogate's office at White Plains to-day brought to light a curious freak of a somewhat eccentric man. Mr. McKnight died this month and left sealed instructions concerning his funeral. He directed that he should be buried in a plain wooded box with rope handles, and that his body should be taken to the Sleepy Hollow Cemetery in an express wagon.

These wishes were partly followed. He was buried in a plain wooded box, but it was stained to represent black walnut. Rope handles were put upon… but they were wound with ribbons, so that the whole presented a respectable appearance. The express wagon was dispensed with the box being put into a hearse and so taken to the cemetery.

The will disposes of an estate of about $15,000. It was made March 18, 1895, and citations returnable May 16 have been issued. He gives his wife the income from the property during her life, and at her death the estate is to be divided between his son William, daughter Florence, and his stepdaughter, Sarah W. Armstrong. He was an upholsterer, and left his tools to his son.

—*New York Times*
April 28, 1896

PAGE 116

Hunt For A Wild Man
Searchers Were Armed And Had Ambulance With Them

MOUNT VERNON- A searching party consisting of Policemen Grant, Riley, and Bellesheim, Gilbert Angevine, Fred Curtis, Harry Anderson, Thomas Hitchcock, H. D. Whittle and others made an exhaustive search for a wild man who is haunting the woods and graveyards near Bronxville. The men were mounted on bicycles and had with them the patrol wagon and ambulance, and each man was heavily armed.

They met more than a dozen persons who had seen the wild man, with the iron band about his waist and wrists and a chain clanking as he ran. Patrick Connelly, coachman for Frank R. Chambers at Crow's Nest, ran into a crouching figure near the barn. A man, nearly naked, with matted hair and glaring eyes, sprang at him, and, throwing up his bare arms, exclaimed: "Down, wretch! Aren't you afraid of the king?" The coachman yelled and ran into the barn. He returned with other servants, armed with pitchforks, to capture the man, but he had disappeared in the dense underbrush. The wild man was also seen by three little boys who were nearly frightened out of their wits.

—*Hornellsville Weekly Tribune*
September 3, 1897

DIGGING HIS OWN GRAVE.

Digging His Own Grave
Charles Miller To Be Hypnotized And Buried Twenty-four Hours

CORTLAND- The sight of a man digging his own grave is an unusual one in this village and crowds of people have thronged the street in the vicinity of Warren & Tanner's store this afternoon watching the preparatory arrangements for burying Charles Miller alive to-night.

He will be placed in a hypnotic state by Dr. Corborne, a hypnotist who has succeeded in interesting several of Cortland's prominent physicians, and they will make an examination of the subject before his resurrection. He will be placed in casket and buried six feet in the earth and will remain there for twenty-four hours, when he will be taken up. Quite a little comment is being made over the matter and some citizens are very indignant that the officials should permit it. They claim that it is sacrilegious and a sin: others claim that it is simply a scientific demonstration and that if a person is willing to allow himself to be the subject they have no objections, but will watch the proceedings and results with interest.

—*Syracuse Post Standard*
October 20, 1899

Wants To Sell His Blood
Bellevue Has An Offer From A Second Man, Who Says He Is Poor.

NEW YORK- Several weeks ago a man came to Bellevue Hospital and said that he was penniless and in great want, but could get no work, and he and his wife were on the verge of starvation. He said that as he was in perfect physician condition the idea had occurred to him that he might make a few dollars by selling his blood to an invalid. Publicity was given to his strange offer and some charitably disposed persons saw that his distress was relieved.

It came to light later, however, that the man was a fugitive from justice and thoroughly undeserving. He received considerable money before it was learned that he was a criminal. Another man is now anxious to dispose of some of his blood. Yesterday W. E. O'Rourke Superintendent of Bellevue Hospital received the following letter:

—*Cornwall*
July 11, 1900

Letter

Mr. Superintendent of Bellevue Hospital, New York City
Dear Sir, I am a very poor man, strong and stout, in good health, but I can get no work, and I don't know how I shall make my living so I think as I am very full blooded I will sell sum of my blood to a sick person that needs good blood. I would go to any city where the sick lives or any place in this country where the sick person is at under Doctor's care. Please notify the other hospital Superintendents who would know where there is sum other sick persons is the city or sum where else. I am ready to go now or any time, but of course I have got no money to go nor board myself, and of course I must be paid for my blood for it is good blood.
Respectfully yours truly,

Citto Bauer
Care of Post Office. Cornwall-on-the-lindson

—*New York Times*
July 13, 1900

Girl Haunted A Jail
Said To Have Been In Love With A Prisoner. Denied At Her Uncle's

WHITE PLAINS- Keepers at the county jail have been much mystified for several days by a girl haunting the neighborhood of the prison. It is said she is in love with Joseph Greely, a young man who is held on a charge of grand larceny committed in Peekskill. The girl who was taken into custody last night came from New York as soon as she heard of Greely's arrest, and since then has been prowling about the jail in the daytime and at night sleeping in fields and in barns in the vicinity.

No one could speak to her for she ran away whenever anybody approached, and was only captured after a pursuit. She seemed a mere child. She said her name was Sarah Farrell, and that she was a niece of Thomas Broderick of 232 West Twenty-sixth Street. She was arraigned before Justice Caperon to-day, and Broderick was in court. He told the Justice that he would give the girl over to the Society for the Prevention of Cruelty to Children, and he was allowed to take her away with that understanding.

At the address given it was found last night, that the number was not the right one, but Mr. Broderick's home was found at 352 in the same street. He occupies the rooms in the basement, and the family appeared to be in a state of considerable excitement last night. Angry voices were heard. A man who said he was a member of the family declared that the girl had long been wayward, but he said there was no truth in the story that she was in love with a prisoner, and they had never heard the name of Greely.

"She is too young to love anybody except her parents," he said. She is not yet thirteen years old. She is a half orphan and lives with her father and step-mother in this city. The man refused to give the address. The girl, he said, had run away from home just a week before and wanted to support herself. She had no money

when recaptured, and had probably spent all she had on rail road fare to White Plains. Mr. Broderick had brought her to the city, the man said, and had turned her over to her father, who had taken her away and would as a punishment have her committed to some strict disciplinary institution, although she had yet been turned over to the Gerry Society, and it is not likely she would be.

—*New York Times*
July 14, 1900

New York's Biggest Woman Dead

NEW YORK- Mrs. Anna Feld, forty-five years old, said to be New York's heaviest woman, who weighed 420 pounds, dropped dead in the street last evening near her home, at Eleventh Avenue and One Hundred and Eighty-seventh Street. A mounted policeman saw the woman's body laying in the street. He asked some men who were near by to help him move the body. Among the men who volunteered was John Feld, the woman's husband. Death was caused by fatty degeneration of the heart.

—*New York Times*
January 9, 1901

EXTRA! EXTRA!

The unofficial heaviest woman to live was Carol Yager (1960-1994) of Flint, MI., who at 5 ft. 7 ins., was estimated to have weighed more than 1600 lbs at her peak.

Strange Form Of Hysteria
Woman's Liking For Hospital Takes Her Often To Bellevue

NEW YORK- What is thought to be a peculiar form of hysteria, the liking for hospitals and for rides in ambulances is believed by the physicians at Bellevue

Hospital to be responsible for the third appearance at the institution in two days of Della Coyne, twenty-eight years old, a domestic, who says she lives at 150 West Thirty-third Street.

The woman was first admitted to the hospital on Thursday, when she walked into the reception room and asked to be treated for nervousness. Friday morning she was discharged as cured, in the afternoon a Flower Hospital ambulance rolled into the hospital grounds, and the Coyne woman was in it. According to the surgeon in charge the woman was suffering from hysteria. She was kept in the institution until yesterday, when she was again discharged at noon.

Not two hours later a call was received at Bellevue Hospital for an ambulance from Thirty-fourth Street and Second Avenue. Dr. Hogan responded. On a doorstep he found the Coyne woman. She was for the third time taken to the institution and again placed in a ward. The woman told the physicians yesterday afternoon that as soon as she started to walk away from the hospital, she is constantly thinking about it, and is not satisfied until an ambulance is summoned and she is taken back to the hospital.

—*New York Times*
September 7, 1902

CHAPTER 6 PECULIAR PEOPLE

Minister Resigns In Order To Read Papers

SYRACUSE- The Rev. C. H. Wetherbee, a Baptist minister of Holland Patent, has retired from the ministry in order further to indulge his passion for reading periodicals. He takes 126 papers and the reading of them requires so much time that he had to give up preaching.

—*Milwaukee Journal*
January 19, 1903

Boy Aged 11 Found Guilty Of Manslaughter

NEW YORK- At the age of 11 years Pietro Aquazza, a child of the tenements, yesterday was found guilty of manslaughter and a maximum penalty is fifteen years in prison. He was accused of throwing a brick from the roof of a house where he lived and killing Ambrose Kerrigan, a child 3 years old, who was playing in the yard. The mother of the dead child said she had warned Pietro, and the jury decided that he was capable. Little Pietro wept bitterly until told that efforts would be made to have the house of refuge or some other institution named instead of state prison. Sentence was deferred until Tuesday.

—*Milwaukee Journal*
January 23, 1903

Circus People Seeking Jobs
How "Human Flies" And Glass Eaters Spend Winter

NEW YORK- Within the past week a peculiar class of people had flocked into New York, "human flies," who walk on ceilings, daring horsemen and women, reckless trapeze performers, acrobats, clowns, and men who eat glass, swallow bayonets, and fondle venomous snakes; for the circus season had ended, and these folks who disport themselves strangely for the public that must be amused, have been thrown out of their regular employment.

While many of these freaks and performers are well paid, few of them have laid by enough money to support them during the winter months. Therefore, as soon as their tents have been folded and the animals taken to their Winter quarters, these attaches of the tented shows look for something to do. Almost any day one may run across some of them in the agencies that provide specialists for all kinds of shows. There are always new vaudeville troupes that must be made up, and frequently a man or woman who can do a good turn can find a place with a company that is appearing in a play. If the play as originally written does not have a part for such a person, if he or she be a really good "artist," a place is made. Then there are the hundreds of museums all over the country that are always on the lookout for something rare. So the performer or the freak does not have a great deal of trouble in "booking" for the winter months.

Another class that is thrown into the cities when the season of the circus closes is composed of those who travel with the tented shows but are not part of them—the "red lame" and toy balloon vendors, and the less vociferous but more dreaded pickpockets, confidence men, and "shell game" operators. They are ever busy, too. When they come to town they seek the rendezvous of fellows of their ilk and ply their trade whenever and wherever possible, but the brightest and most promising day for them is when Spring comes, and the circuses start again on their tours through the country.

—*New York Times*
October 11, 1903

St. Ronan's Well Hermit Dead
Odd Character Of Flushing Bay Died From The Cold

FLUSHING- Oscar Himman, known as the hermit of St. Ronan's Well, was found dead in his shanty on the sand dunes near the romantic well yesterday afternoon by a party of friends who called to see how the old man was standing the cold weather. St. Ronan's Well occupies a promontory facing the Flushing Bay about half a mile outside of the village of Flushing.

A mansion years ago crowned the heights of the bluff, but it was totally destroyed by fire one night. Local tradition says that the old well was haunted by the spirit of a beautiful young woman who committed suicide by jumping into the well rather than prove untrue to her lover and marry a man selected for her by her family. For years the place was shunned, but the cutting away of the forest that crowned the bluff and the running of trolley cars within sight of the place gradually dispelled the tradition, and of late years sand diggers began cutting away the hill.

Many years ago Himman built a shanty on the hill and made his home there. He is reputed to have been wealthy at one time, but lost his fortune in speculations. He received small remittances from a source which he never disclosed, and he occasionally did small jobs about the bay. He was well educated, but was never known to talk concerning his family affairs.

When the searching party arrived at his hovel yesterday they found the place closed, and forced open the back door. The prostrate form of the old hermit was discovered lying dead in his bead. He had probably perished from the cold. Himman was about seventy years old. The body was turned over to Coroner Ruoff.

—*New York Times*
February 12, 1904

Boy Pirate Buries Treasure

WILLIAMSBURG- Emulating the example of his favorite Captain Kidd, who was wont after a plundering expedition to secrete the treasure he could not use, Ryman Ratsky, 12 years old, use this seller of an old tenement house in Williamsburg as a place in which to bury $460 in cash and $300 dollars in checks which the police say he stole from the provision store of Isadora Cohen, 916 Moore Street, Williamsburg, yesterday morning.

It was only after an extended search that the police were able to locate the youthful Kidd at Coney Island, where with his chief lieutenant Morris Weiss, 13 years old, he was holding high sail to the sleep envy of a score of other small boys, who followed him open-eyed at his prodigality. He succeeded in spending $20 dollars before the enemy captured him.

Ratsky, who is familiar with the inside of the Cohen store, sneaked in the rear of the place yesterday morning the police allege, and seizing the bundles of money in checks that he found on a shelf got away without being noticed. When the loss was discovered it was remembered and, his penchant for buccaneering exploits being recalled, the police were asked to find him.

He insisted that he had buried his treasure in the sand of the beach and took the detectives from one place to another for the better part of two hours, pretending not to be able to find the cache. After he had been given a taste of the "third degree" his memory proved better and then he led them to the house where the money was found.

When Policeman Green found him he was about to cater into negotiations for the purchase of the baby elephant at Bogstok's which pleased his fancy. Weiss was also arrested and is being held in the charge of vagrancy. Ratsky is accused of grand lar-

ceny. He lives at Throop Avenue and Bartlett Street, Williamsburg.

—*La Crosse Tribune*
March 9, 1906

Mackenzie Is A Giant
Weighs 328
And Is Seven Feet Two Inches Tall.
An Advance Agent.

SYRACUSE- Major R. B. Mackenzie, known throughout the United States, Canada and Europe as the "Celtic Giant," is in Syracuse to-day. He is the advance agent of Barney Gilmore, who comes to the Bastable next week. Major Mackenzie is the second man in statue in the world, being 7 feet, 2 inches in height, finely proportional and weighing 328 pounds. His only rival is Macknow, the Russian giant, who is a few inches taller.

Major Mackenzie was born in Canada thirty-two years ago of Scotch-Irish parentage. His father was a native-born Highlander and his mother a Dublin woman. The major spent most of his early days in Ireland. He enlisted in the Gordon Highlanders and did service in Africa, where he won his title. He has many musical accomplishments, being especially skilled in the Scotch and Irish bagpipes, the harp and the violin.

Major Mackenzie has traveled throughout the United States, Europe, Australia, New Zealand and other parts of the world and has twice appeared by royal command before King Edward and at Washington to President Roosevelt.

—*Syracuse Herald*
December 17, 1906

EXTRA! EXTRA!

The tallest documented man in history was is Robert Pershing Wadlow. He was born in Illinois, on February 22, 1918, and when he was last measured, on June 27, 1940, he was 8 ft. 11.1 ins. tall.

Call Him Most Anything

SYRACUSE- Man with peculiar name is again in town. "The mysterious man of the Warner," as he is popularly known to the hotel people in this city, arrived at that hotel this morning from Atlanta, Ga. The man of mystery comes to this city about five times a year and always stops at this hotel. Each time he arrives he registers but the person who can solve his handwriting has not yet appeared and his name is still unknown. His name can be read for Smith or Brown or White or any other one with five letters. The hotel clerks call him by all of these names and they do not know which is right.

CHAPTER 6 PECULIAR PEOPLE

Mr. Smith etc., declined to give a *Herald* man his name this morning—beyond saying, "Look at the register." He was willing to talk politics, however, and told about conditions in the South. "In the Southern States Hearst Hisgen and the whole Independence crowd are a huge joke," he said. "Bryan is unpopular for a Democratic candidate because of his inconsistency on the negro question, in the North the Nebraskan is pronigger and in the South he talks against the blacks. I never have been a Republican, but I guess I'll have to vote for Taft, as there is no choice left me." Mr. Smith left later in the morning for New York. Each time that he stops at the hotel he registers from a different city. He usually picks some place in California or Washington.

—*Syracuse Herald*
August 4, 1908

Wrote His Own Obituary
Cyrus Clark, Who Died Yesterday, Left One Blank In It.

NEW YORK- Cyrus Clark, for many years President of the West End Association, and prominent in the development of the west side, died yesterday in his home, 327 West Seventy-sixth Street, of paralysis, in his seventy-ninth year. He was stricken on May 15. There was a reoccurrence of the attack on Wednesday.

Mr. Clark was known as a very methodical man, a phase of his character which was emphasized by his preparation of his own obituary notice with the date of his death left blank. This blank his son filled yesterday. The notice that Mr. Clark had written says:

"Cyrus Clark was born Sept. 18, 1830, in the town of Sardinia, Erie County, N. Y., and his parents moved to Buffalo soon afterward, in which city he received his early education. In 1849 Mr. Clark came to New York and entered the employ of Clark, Southworth, & Co., silk merchants, where he stayed five years, and then started for himself under the name of Vincent Clark & Co. At the end of ten years he retired from the silk business, having invested his money in real estate to good advantage.

"After spending three years in Europe studying civic conditions Mr. Clark returned to this city in 1870 and took up his residence on the west side. He caused the first bill to be introduced into the Legislature to exempt mortgages from taxation, and was President of the west End Association for fifteen years. He was a member of the Union League Club for forty-six years, and was vice-president of the club for one term. He is survived by two sons and three daughters."

—*New York Times*
May 25, 1909

EXTRA! EXTRA!

In 1900, 42% of the workforce was in farming.

Got $60,000 Fortune By Picking Rags

**Story Of Monaghan Family's
Strange Life Revealed By
Brother's Death In Stable.
All Vowed Never To Wed.
But Joseph Broke The Pledge.
Breach Healed Over
His Coffin In A Stall.
Sister The Treasurer.**

MASPETH- The history of a strange family, how they have lived as ragpickers and accumulated a fortune amounting to at least $60,000, how one of them lived in a stable and was buried from there, was brought out yesterday by the probating of the will of Joseph Monaghan of Maspeth, L.I., by John T. Robinson, an attorney of Elmhurst.

The family, which now consists of two brothers and a sister, another sister having died, met on Wednesday for the first time in several years in the stable where Joseph's funeral was held. Nearly 700 people surrounded the stable at the time, for the Monaghans and their eccentricities are well known in the community. The coffin reposed in one of the stalls and candles were placed on the partitions. There were even flowers distributed around the stable. In this queer situation the two remaining brothers and the one sister clasped hands and effected reconciliation, which was the closing incident in a quarrel which had lasted several years.

It was nearly fifty years ago that Patrick Monaghan came to America from Ireland and settled in lower Manhattan. He brought his wife and three children, Patrick, Jr., John, and Alice. Afterward there were born to him a daughter and a son, Margaret and Joseph. After living in this country for a decade the father died. The children at that time gathered around his coffin and formed a strange compact. They agreed always to live together, always to work together, and never to marry. Alice, the oldest child, was to have charge of the money.

About twenty years ago the family moved to Maspeth in the Newtown section of Queens County. The mother died soon after. The vocation of the Monaghans was ragpicking and scavenging. They worked hard and faithfully, and all the money thus made was turned over to Alice. Much of the income she invested in real estate they owned. It was not long after the family moved to Maspeth that the first break came. Joseph decided to get married. He moved away from his brothers and sisters after he had taken this step, but although he had displeased his brothers and sisters he did not succeed in pleasing his wife, because he insisted on continuing to turn over most of his income to Alice.

In the end the two found it impossible to live together and they separated. Mrs. Joseph Monaghan and the child, Rosie, live at 2036 Second Avenue Manhattan. When Joseph left his wife he and his brother Patrick went to live in the stable of a house they owned. They rented the house. Patrick owned several horses which had to be kept somewhere, and the brothers slept in a stall between them. Here it was that Joseph died.

About five years ago there was trouble again in the family, this time over money. The case was taken into court and Alice was compelled to divide the estate so that each one got his share. Margaret died soon after this, and she felt so unfriendly toward Alice that she left her only $5. She thought that the law compelled her to leave her sister something. The rest of her estate she divided in her will between her three brothers. Since then the family has been separated. Alice, now 62 years old, has lived alone; Patrick 60 years old, has lived in the stable with Joseph, while John had lived in one room of a house that he owns. Patrick is nearly blind, but he continues to do a great deal of work. Joseph had been unlucky with his money, and in the end was worth less than the others. He leaves only about $2,000 of which $500 goes to his widow and the rest to his brother Patrick.

The crowd which collected at Joseph's funeral had the strange experience of see-ing this curious family collect and become reconciled with each other. Even Joseph's widow was received with the others in the stable where the two brothers have lived for so long. The will was filed in the Queen County Surrogate's Court and the question of admitting it to probate will come up on July 13. "It is impossible to tell the value of the property until the parties appear in court," said John T. Robinson, the attorney, who filed the will. "But the value of the combined estate is undoubtedly quite a sum." Mr. Robinson also filed Margaret's will. Ex-Judge George Burr of Maspeth has long taken a friendly interest in the family, and he is the executor of the will. The wife, it is said, is satisfied with her share of $500.

—*New York Times*
July 1, 1909

Wild Man Fights Police
Found Frothing At The Mouth And Barking In Harlem

MANHATTAN- The sight of a man froth-ing at the mouth, baring savagely, and snapping at persons in the street attracted the attention of Policeman Mullen of the West 100th Street Police Station at 103rd Street and Amsterdam Avenue last night. He tried to hold the man down, and his hands were scratched, and he was badly beaten when Policeman Rouse ran to his assistance.

The prisoner was taken to the station house and there recognized as the man who had been found by Policeman Clarke at

Riverside Drive and 108th Street about a month ago, chewing the bark from trees and frightening women by his wild behavior.

The name of the man could not be learned at that time, and he was unable to give any account of himself last night. He was sent to Bellevue on the previous occasion after a fight with the police in the station house. He declared at the time that he had been bitten by a dog, but the Bellevue doctors said that he was suffering from alcoholism. Last night he was taken to Bellevue once more by Dr. Du Bois in a J. Hood Wright Hospital ambulance.

—*New York Times*
July 4, 1909

Wild Man Seen In Woods Near Rainbow Lake
Mysterious Stranger Spreads Terror Through Community.
Sheriff Had Been Notified.
Hollow Tree Used As A Home By Strange Character Who Is Believed To Be An Escaped Lunatic.

RAINBOW LAKE- There is great excitement at Rainbow Lake, some thirty miles south of Malone, on the Adirondack branch of the New York Central, over the appearance of a wild man. It is said that some two weeks ago the man jumped from a train and made for the woods, where he has been hiding. His lodge has been found in a hollow tree about half a mile from the railroad station.

Many chickens have mysteriously disappeared and numerous persons have been frightened by the appearance of a long-haired man. Sheriff Steenbergy has been notified. The man is supposed to be an escaped lunatic. To-day Sheriff Steenbergy received an additional letter asking him to capture the man, who has terrorized the community for miles around.

—*Syracuse Post Standard*
November 18, 1909

Little Girl Under Strange Spell Acts Like A Savage
Adopted Daughter Of An Owasco Couple Committed To
A Rochester Institution Because Of Her Peculiar Conduct.
Her Parentage Kept A Secret.

OWASCO- A young girl of Owasco, 8 years old, was committed to a Rochester Institution by Justice Pearson a few days ago. The foster parents are childless, and about six years ago they adopted the child from an orphan asylum said to be located in Oneida. After she had been in the family for a few years she began to act strangely. She would go down on her hands and knees, it is said, run and grovel in the road and bark, snap, and snarl like a dog, and when angered she would chase the inmates of the house about and would badly frighten them. She evidenced a love of dogs rather than children and dolls. This was thought at first to be evidence of bad temper, but all efforts to control the child or change her mode of life were unsuccessful, and she gradually became it is alleged, more and more like a dog in her habits.

When she arrived at school age she was sent to the district school, but her actions were so unusual that the teachers and pupils refused to attend school with her. Becoming frightened, her foster parents sought medical advice, and an examination of the child by physicians brought out the fact that she was controlled by pre-natal influences and that before her birth her mother had been badly frightened by a dog. As the child became older her habits more closely followed that a dog and she seemed to lose all control of her temper and was ungovernable.

The foster parents were so badly scared that they refused to keep the child any longer and sought the advice of Justice Pearson, who examined the child while in one of her spells. He advised her commitment to an institution and the advice was followed. She was then committed to a semi-private institution for ungovernable children, but her antics so badly scared the

matron and the attendants that they refused to keep the child and the Justice was compelled to receive her back and she was committed to the Rochester Institution. Who the child's parents are, or where her actual home is, her foster parents and those familiar with the case refuse to disclose.

—*Syracuse Post Standard*
January 10, 1910

She Keeps
A Hundred Cats
New York Woman Known As
Pied Piperess Of Catdom

NEW YORK- Far from the terrors of civilization there dwells in Grand Street a century coterie of cats at No. 460, known as "the house of 100 cats and 900 lives."

It is not an uncommon sight to see Mrs. Swiss going to market with two score or more of the felines at her heels, and she really enjoys the distinction of being styled the Pied Piperess of catdom. For ten years she has taken the entire output of scrap meat from two butchers near her home, and this she always cooks before it is served to the cats. Most of the animals are waifs or have been rescued from mistreatment by Mrs. Swiss. "She should be a humane officer," says her husband.

—*Syracuse Herald*
January 16, 1910

Strange Acting Man Fells Fordham Students

NEW YORK- "The Lord has sent me to save your soul. I am appointed to this mission," said a huge stranger, of rough dress and wild manner, to the students of Fordham College to-day, as they were pouring from recitations. Without further explanation he felled the nearest student with a blow on the head from his heavy carpet bag.

The students tried to rush the stranger. He felled six of the in succession with his carpet bag, and then knocked out a special officer who came to the rescue. A mounted policeman was repulsed on the first attack by a blow on his horse's nose, but he came back again at a gallop the second time and bowled the missionary over.

In the police station the prisoner gave his name as John Roth of this city. He was held for examination into his sanity.

—*Syracuse Post Standard*
January 20, 1910

Willie Eats 'Em Alive
Bosco Of The freak Museum Not The Only Worm Exterminator

MIDDLETOWN- W. B. Proctor the well known soap millionaire imputed a part of his success to his soap's popularity among children. Mr. Proctor claims that habits of scrupulous cleanliness could be formed in children if, at first, they were paid to bathe. He had at the tip a number of amusing

anecdotes about the extraordinary mercenary character of the small boy.

One of these anecdotes concerned a little boy who came to his mother one day for a nickel. "Oh," said the lady, "be industrious and earn your money, I am tired of always giving to you." The youngster departed in thoughtful silence. Thereafter for some time, he did not make a single demand for cash. His pleased mother discovered the reason for this obedience late one afternoon, when in a secluded part of her garden, she found her little son standing in the center of an appreciative crowd of urchins.

Directly behind him, quite neatly printed on cardboard and tacked to the arbor; was this announcement:

Willie Jones Will Eat
1 small worm for .... 1 cent
1 large worm for ....2 cents
1 butterfly for.......................2 cents
1 caterpillar.........................3 cents
1 hop toad for.......................5 cents

And the boy his mother plainly saw, was doing a tremendous business.

—*Middletown Orange County Times Press*
July 29, 1910

Psychic Phenomena

An Old Superstition
What An Ancient Mirror Foretold.
The Death Of Mrs. Fullerton.

MIDDLETOWN- Says the Middletown Argus: Country people, and, in fact, a great many town and city folks still cling to old superstitions, and even that "coming events cast their shadow before." A case in point, and one, too, which will go a long way to keep this superstition alive in the minds of those who were present and those who listen to its recital, occurred just before the death of the late Mrs. Ester Fullerton at Slate Hill. Her physician and numerous relatives of the family were seated in a room adjoining the one wherein the aged lady was sleeping, when suddenly a large mirror that had hung against the wall of the room for many years cracked to pieces, and a few minutes after a new glass lamp chimney cracked and fell. It was in the afternoon, and the lamp was not burning.

All the members of the family and the physician also, were deeply impressed when they heard the report and some of those present looked upon the strange phenomenon as a premonition of the early dissolution of Mrs. Fullerton, an event which was verified a short time afterwards.

—*Port Jervis Evening Gazette*
January 13, 1877

The Music Of His Dream
A Violinist Plays A Tune Acquired While In His Sleep

NEW YORK- A well-known violin-player in Warren County, New York, who has played for years for county dances, has a lively dancing tune, greatly admired by all who hear it, that has a queer origin. The player in question never learned music, plays entirely "by ear," and never in his life tried to compose a tune, but he can play any ordinary composition after hearing it once or twice.

One night he dreamed of meeting an old man in the road carrying a violin. In his dream he asked the old fellow to play. He responded with a weird, reel-like sort of jig. The old man played it so nicely that the delighted dreamer asked if he could play another piece, a favorite of the dreamer's own. The old fiddler said he could and played the same piece over again. "No," said the dreamer, 'that's the same tune you played first; give me something else." "All right," said the old man, "I'll give you what you want," and he again played the tune he started off with.

The experience was repeated several times, and at last the dreamer awoke. The impression of the dream was so strong that he could not get the tune out of his mind,

and he arose, got his violin, and after one or two trials reproduced the tune and has played it ever since. He calls it "Bryant's Favorite," after a friend who took a great fancy to the air. No one has found who has ever heard the tune elsewhere, and there seems to be no doubt that there is at least one musical composition that was produced by "unconscious cerebration."

—*Dallas Morning News*
May 13, 1888

Spiritualism In Bradford
An Athletic "Ghost" Who Offered To Lick A Spectator

BRADFORD- Bradford spiritists are all torn up over an exposure made by one of their number at a séance at the house of James Campbell on Congress Place in that city. About twenty members of the local spiritist circle attended the séance and paid $1 each for the privilege of conversing with the deceased individuals who were to come to earth through the influence of Medium Oren Stevens.

The room was darkened, and at the proper time a tall, white figure appeared at the cabinet opening. The white spirit made a speech and disappeared. Then a baseball ghost, who said he had been killed in a hot game in Tennessee some years ago, appeared and jumped about the rooms, showing how he threw his curves. The phenomenal pitcher gave a specimen of his style in the presence of W. L. Dudley, a spectator. Dudley clutched the ghost and found it to be a very active individual still

in the flesh. Dudley is a muscular man but the spirit put a stranglehold on the investigator and got back to his cabinet.

Great confusion followed, and in the excitement Stevens reappeared and said he was a southern gentleman and could lick the man that grabbed him. He thus acknowledged that he had impersonated the ghost of the ball-player, and still there were believers present who joined him in denouncing Dudley. Peace was finally restored and the next day the medium left town. Dudley will have him arrested for obtaining money under false pretenses if he returns to Bradford. Stevens came last fall from Indianapolis, and has lived in clover since. He is a Lilly Dale star, and will probably appear there in his specialties during the summer.

—Olean Democrat
July 17, 1894

Say They Saw A Miracle
A Picture Of The Virgin Said To Have Appeared On A Window Blind

TARRYTOWN- Mrs. Mary Malvelle, a simple, pious old woman, lay dying just three weeks ago in her little frame house at Tarrytown, within a few doors of St. Teresa's church, which she attended during the many years of her widowhood. Around her were grouped her children, several of her oldest friends and neighbors, and two sisters of the Franciscan order.

Sister Clare sat at the elbow of the half conscious woman, whispering words of comfort. The room, which was on the ground floor, was darkened except for the light that came from the room adjoining. The bed on which Mrs. Malvelle lay faced a little to the right of the one window that looked out on the street. The ill-fitting Holland blind was drawn down and lapped closely over the edge of the window frame. The clock ticking away the few remaining hours of the old woman's life, pointed 3:05. Then the men and women in the room say they became aware of a remarkable presence. Over the part of the blind that covered the frame of the window, they say, there seemed to spread a white cloud that grew and deepened as the minutes wore on. Then instantly in bright colors, they say, there shone out a figure which all of them knew.

There, complete, distinct and clear, they say they saw a picture of the Immaculate Conception. The virgin stood with hands extended. All gazed speechless and silent in wonderment. The two sisters—cultivated, refined women—were, like the others, confounded and deprived of the power of speaking. When they recovered their presence of mind they hurried into the next room in the hope of finding some explanation. There on the wall was the figure of the Virgin Mary, but in this painting her hands were clasped in prayer. They say they covered the picture and turned down the light, but that the wondrous appearance in the bedroom only shone out the brighter.

Neighbors were brought in, no word of preparation being spoken, and as they entered the room they stared and pointed to the picture. On the outer side of the blind nothing could be seen. All means of solving the mystery were tried, but each failed, and at last the neighbors accepted it as a visitation from heaven and waited until as the day dawned, the vision faded away. Once during the night the dying woman had awakened. Her eyes rested on the figure. "There is the picture of the virgin," she murmured, "but it is not as I ever saw it before. The face looks sweeter. Now I know that I shall die." Thus speaking she sank into a stupor that ended only in her death two days afterwards.

Once again the figure appeared, the next night, but this time only for a few moments. All who saw it agree that it was small, but was wonderfully sharp and clear in its outlines. When Mrs. Malvelle was buried her daughter cut the curtain into many small pieces and distributed them among their friends.

—*Dallas Morning News*
April 7, 1895

Sightings of the Virgin Mary continue today, as each year hundreds of sightings are reported from around the world.

Saw Friends In Heaven
**Peculiar Experience Of A Woman
Who Thought Herself Dying.
John Hazeltine Saw Circus.
Dr. Hitchcock
Tells Of A Strange Scene.
Three Plainly Witnessed
White Form Of A Woman
Who Had Been Dead Several Years.
Dying College Man Made Some
Confessions, But Recovered.
Manning Heard The Undertaker
Refuse To Bury Him.
Stories Of Death Bed Incidents.**

SYRACUSE- Those who callings bring them into contact with the more serious phases of life meet with many incidents which do not often find their way into print, but which are interesting, pathetic or sometimes hideous. How will I meet death? is a question which most everyone has asked himself at some time. Will I meet it bravely without special incident, will I suffer untold agonies, and, in short, what will be my feelings when I am experiencing death?

Many of the Syracuse physicians and clergymen can relate interesting incidents and scenes in connection with deathbeds. "Although the fear of death," said Dr. A. B. Kinne to a Post Standard reporter, "is the most pronounced dread of the human race, it is taken away absolutely by severe or continued pain. Young people of course hate to die worse than old. The most peculiar incident that was ever called to my attention in connection with death was that of a lady 96 years of age who had never been sick much, but yet wanted to die. At 4 o'clock one afternoon she began failing and called her friends and nurses about her and to all appearances was dying. Her pulse left her, but she could talk. She told those around her bedside that she could see her friends in Heaven and seemed to have a vision of the Golden City. The peculiar part of this case was that the woman did not die at that time, but lived for six weeks afterward and all the time insisted that she had seen her husband, who had died seventeen years before."

Saw A Circus

John Hazeltine had an experience some years ago which he does not want to pass through again, although it has an amusing circumstance connected with it. He was fishing off a dock near Plattsburgh, Clinton County, when he hooked an immense pickerel. The fish was so large that Mr. Hazeltine in his efforts to pull it a shore slipped and fell into the water and was nearly drowned. It is said that drowning persons recall in an instant everything that has occurred during their lives, Mr. Hazeltine's vision of his past life, however, was limited to a circus performance. He says he saw Barnum's three ringed circus in full operation. Elephants, monkeys, camels, horses, trapeze performers and clowns passed before his eyes and his delight was only interrupted by being pulled out of the water by Wealthy Wascott, a minister who was passing by. At this time Mr. Hazeltine's hand remained clasped around the fish pole and the fish was landed at last. Hazeltine says it weighed five and three-quarters pounds. He had it stuffed and still keeps it as a memento of the time he involuntarily went to the circus.

"The will power has a great deal to do with death and the way one meets it," said Dr. Ely Van de Walker the other day. "I have known many cases where a man's physical condition was much as to have cased his death, but he lived for some time by sheer force of will." Death itself is and must be absolutely painless, although the state preceding death may not be so. The fear of death is instinctive as a mean of self preservation the same as a fear of physical pain. The latter in some cases is stronger than fear of death, as there are doubtless many despondent persons who would end their existence but for the fear of the pain it would cause them.

Alive But Thought Dead

A guest at the St. Cloud Hotel tells a hair raising story about a commercial traveler named Manning whom he knows well and who had often been in Syracuse. A few months ago Manning was taken sick while at a hotel in the West and he was thought to be dead. An undertaker was called to embalm the body and prepare it for burial, but noticed that the body did not cool off

and refused to have anything to do with it. For three successive days the undertaker refused to embalm the body, although the physician had declared the man to be dead.

Finally Manning came to life and was able to relate his experiences. He was fully aware of what was going on around him and was in terrible agony for fear the undertaker would inject embalming fluid into his veins and he knew that it would be all up with him then. Manning is now able to be about his business and to relate his experience. There are several instances of people on their death beds who seemed to have supernatural visions. It is seldom, however, that their attendants see the same visions. Rev. J. E. Rhondes of Canastota was talking with a Post-Standard reporter recently. "I always take stories of that kind," said he, "with a grain of salt." Rev. Dr. Luke Hitchcock, formerly of the Methodist Book Publishing Concern, whom I well know and whose word is beyond question, told me a strange incident which happened when his father died. There were in the room besides Dr. Hitchcock and the dying man two ladies.

Saw His Dead Mother

"Just as Mr. Hitchcock breathed his last Dr. Hitchcock saw the white form of his mother, who had died some years before, walk to the head of the bed and lay her hand on his father's head. Dr. Hitchcock said nothing about it at the time, thinking that the vision was the product of his imagination. Later, however, he mentioned his experience to the two ladies who were in the room and was surprised to learn that they had also distinctly seen the same white form go and lay its hand on the dying man's head."

"I once attended a case," said a well known physician, "where a young man was thought to be dying of typhoid fever. He was the son of a clergyman and had been attending one of the large colleges. He had been brought up in the strict old-fashioned way and for all his parents knew was a model son. Just as he was thought to be breathing his last he raised up in bed and began confessing his sins. Imagining that he was dead and was before the recording angel. His confession was a revelation to his parents and showed them that their model boy had been on of the "sports" at the college. It is interesting to note that the boy got well but he was not allowed to return to college."

There is no doubt that many strange incidents have occurred to death beds. Physicians who are inclined to be materialistic say that everything can be attributed to natural causes or an over excited imagination. Many, however, believe that the day of the supernatural had not passed and that men of to-day as well as of old "see visions and dream dreams."

—*Syracuse Post Standard*
July 9, 1899

Fortune Teller's Revelation
On Strength Of It, Woman Has Son-in-law Arrested On Charge Of Theft.

YONKERS- Harry Smith of 26 Warburton Avenue was held by Judge Kellogg to-day upon a charge of grand larceny, made by his stepmother, Mrs. Ella Smith of 240 New Main Street. His wife was also arrested, but was not held.

The property stolen was in cash and jewelry. When Mrs. Smith discovered her loss she went to a fortune teller, who told her that the cards showed a great financial loss that the money had been taken by a dark man who had given it to a light woman, who was slightly older than he and that they had gone on a journey. It also happens that the young man is dark that his wife is light, and a little bit older than he, and that at the time they had gone on a trip to Saugerties. This settled it in Mrs. Smith's opinion. She went to the court, obtained a warrant, and the arrest was made. On the stand Mrs. Smith declared that she had not suspected the young man until it was suggested to her by the fortune teller. She admitted she had nothing to back up her belief except the fortune teller's allegation.

The counsel for the prisoners surprised every one by calling the fortune teller to the stand. She admitted the visit of Mrs. Smith, and repeated what Mrs. Smith had testified to as to what had passed between them. She was asked if she had not had some conversation with Mrs. Smith and admitted she had, and that Mrs. Smith hinted at the young man during the conversation before the cards were consulted. No other evidence confirmatory of Mrs. Smith's charge against her son-in-law was added.

—*New York Times*
July 13, 1900

In 1890, the average annual income for a family of four was $380.

Harris Trial Again Delayed

Negroes Confident That The Defendant Is A "Cunjah Doctah"

NEW YORK- The continued illness of Juror William Abbott caused the fourth postponement of the trial of the negro, Arthur Harris, charged with the murder of Policeman Robert J. Thorpe, in the Criminal Branch of the Supreme Court, yesterday.

A larger number of colored residents of the

west side were present in court than at any previous day and the opinion among them that Harris is a "cunjah doctah" was widespread. "Do you think Harris is a witch doctor?" an old negro on crutches softly singing to himself was asked. "Looks dat way fo' sho'" was the reply. "Ef dat niggah ain't a voodoo man den he's might nigh it. Some'n s doin,' I reckon, or dis hyuh case 'ud done been tried." If juror Abbott is still ill to-day, a new jury will be drawn.

—*New York Times*
October 25, 1900

Because Of Premonition
Mr. Beach Moved Out Of His House.
Last Night It Was On Fire twice And Caused A Train Of Casualties In Town.

LYONS- A tenant, house No. 55 Elmer Street, owned by Thomas O'Blalley, was discovered on fire twice last night, the first time between 6 and 7 o'clock and the second time at 10 o'clock.

The home was occupied by William A. Beach, who because of a premonition his wife had began moving yesterday to the opposite side of the street. When the second fire was discovered Beach found some oiled waste burning in the second story of the building, and the fire is believed to be of incendiary origin. Hermann F. Ongerer was attending the Freeman's fair when the second alarm sounded and fell in a fit. Charles Rither fell in Canal Street while going to the fire and his right arm was fractured. The damage to the house was $500 and the content $500.

—*Syracuse Evening Herald*
November 16, 1900

Foretold His Own Death

SODUS- The death of Hugh Pound of Williamson, one of the most prominent young men of this community, occurred at 6 o'clock this morning. The deceased attended a party Friday night and made the remark that it was the last time he would

ever dance with his Williamson friends. On Saturday he worked until late at night in his father's store. Sunday he was taken violently ill and grew rapidly worse until this morning when death relieved him. He was 20 years of age. He only survivors are his parents, Mr. and Mrs. William H. Pound.

—*Syracuse Post Standard*
December 12, 1900

Foretold His Own Death
A. L. Floyd Stricken While On The Way To His Brother's Funeral

NEW YORK- In fulfillment of a prophecy made by himself, A. L. Floyd, a Boston cotton manufacturer, was stricken ill in front of 62 Park Avenue late yesterday afternoon and died almost immediately.

There were three brothers, A. J., E. D., and S. D. Floyd, in the cotton manufacturing business. The firm name was Floyd Brothers. The headquarters of the house is at Chauncey Street Boston. A branch is maintained at 190 West Broadway, this city, E. D. Floyd was in charge of the Boston end of the business and S. D. Floyd looked after the New York interest. He lived at West Seventh Street. He became ill last week and died at 5 o'clock Monday morning.

When his brother, A. J. Floyd, fifty-seven years old, heard of the death he was in Boston. "I believe I'll follow him shortly," he said to one of his commercial salesmen, J. C. Shaller. "I will not be surprised if I went this week." Mr. Shaller tried to cheer his employee up and seemed to succeed. Mr. Floyd at once came to this city to attend the funeral, which was held yesterday afternoon at the Church of the Messiah, Park Avenue and Thirty-fourth Street. He was down at the West Broadway office early in the day and was on his way to the funeral services when he was stricken.

So convinced was he that his death was near at hand that he had three sealed envelopes on him when he died, in which he gave minute directions to relatives as to his interests. When he was stricken he was unknown to anyone in the vicinity, and for several hours the police records had him down as "unidentified." Detectives managed to locate Mr. Shaller at the Hotel Manhattan, Shaller made the identification at once. The surviving relatives were notified and they gave orders for the removal of the body to an undertaking shop. The funeral will be arranged to-day. Another brother, Charles O. Floyd dropped dead in Boston within the past year.

—*New York Times*
March 21, 1901

Had Premonition Of Death
Said Five Years Ago He Would Die On Friday Aug. 30

NEW YORK- Joseph Miller, eighty-two years old, who died in Bellevue Hospital on Friday, had a peculiar premonition of the day in which his death would occur.

Five years ago he said he would go on a Friday and on Aug 30. He repeated this declaration three weeks ago, and that was the day on which he died.

Miller's final illness was stomach trouble, coupled with heart disease. He had not been able to work for seventeen years. A granddaughter has been supporting him. His wife is nearly seventy years old. The necessary money for burying the dead man is not forthcoming, and there is a very bitter sorrow in the rear building at 572 East Sixteenth Street, one flight up.

—*New York Time*s
September 1, 1901

Jilted Indian Dies Insane
Had A Premonition When His Brother, A Tribal Chief, Died.

NEW YORK- The full-blooded Indian Evans Bradby who was jilted by a white girl, died early yesterday morning in the insane pavilion of Bellevue Hospital. Bradby came from the reservation at Whitehouse Va., about a year ago and while an assistant steward on the steamboat Priscilla of the Fall River Line fell in love with the daughter of the engineer, who at last had to tell him she could not marry him. It is said that not long afterward he showed signs of mental derangement.

Mrs. Harriet Maxwell Converse says that on May 13th the Indian suddenly shouted that something had happened to his brother, chief of the tribe at Whitehouse, and it was afterward learned that the brother had died at just the hour Bradby had shouted. The regular Indian burial services will be conducted over the body.

—*New York Times*
May 30, 1902

Woman Charges Friend With Witchcraft

NEWARK- Mrs. Annie Lesnik of Newark is charged by Mrs. May Guth, lately her friend, with having administered a brew of tea over which some type of incantation had been held, and which had affected her strangely. Mrs. Guth declares that since drinking he decoction she has lost sense of locality. Mrs. Guth made a charge of witchcraft against Mrs. Lesnik to a justice of the peace, who will hold an examination.

—*Milwaukee Journal*
January 19, 1903

Band Disturbs Spirit Visit
Medium Confronts Opposition At Empire Hall Séance.
"Bob" Ingersoll Is Lauded.
Hailed As Pioneer Of Religious Liberty.
Stories From The Bible Are Branded As Ridiculous.

SYRACUSE- Floating up through the hot, sticky air, the strains from a German street band added a touch of materialism to last night's spiritualist séance at Empire

Hall. F. Cordonik White, the medium from Lilly Dale, N.Y., was no more then launched in his search in the other world for friends of persons present than the seductive strains commenced.

"Does any one present recognize the name of Nehemiah?" inquired the medium, and loud and shrill, louder even than the rumble of the street cars, the clarinet in the band let out a screech. Interest seemed to be about evenly divided between the departed Nehemiah and the band.

In spite of the band, however, which did not appear to interest the really elect, the meeting went along without a hitch. Spirits told their friends how happy they found the other world when suddenly without a minute's warning the medium brought the séance to a close by saying, "Friends I have done enough." The séance was the last thing on the programme, and before it was reached one man in the audience got tired of waiting. "When are the spirits coming?" asked he.

Before the spirit messages commenced a programme consisting of musical selections and addresses was rendered. Mrs. Gertrude Mudge of this city delivered a short address, and Rev. B.F. Austin of Geneva held the memory and deeds of Robert Green Ingersoll up for approval.

Tells Of Minister's Defeat

The great agnostic was lauded as a pioneer of religious liberty in thought and the speaker made many references to Mr. Ingersoll's "digs" at the clergy. Following Mr. Austin, W. H. Bach, editor of The Sun

Flower, the organ of the Spiritualists, tried to prove that the bible was a sort of anti-quated Joe Miller's Joke Book. There were, he said, several things in it that he could not understand. After showing that some of the stories in the bible were ridiculous, from his viewpoint, he told the audience how easily he routed a clergyman who attempted to question Spiritualism. The incident, so he said, took place out in Missouri. Mr. Bach concluded his remarks with the recital of several death bed scenes which he advanced as proof of Spiritualism.

The business of the seventh annual convention of the New York State Association Empire Hall in this city Friday, closed yesterday afternoon with the re-election of all the officers. The meeting place has not been decided upon, but in all probability it will be Syracuse. Meetings will be held this afternoon and evening at Empire Hall and Mr. White will take place in both.

—*Syracuse Post Standard*
June 5, 1904

Dreamed He'd Die
And Did
Electrician Kissed Wife Good-bye
And Went To Death
On Elevated Road

NEW YORK- A premonition of death which John J. Jennings, an electrician employed on the West Side elevated line of the Interborough Road, received in a dream on Thursday night was followed yesterday by his actual death, much as he

had dreamed it would be brought about. Jennings left his home at 246 West One Hundred and Forty-third Street in the morning, kissing his wife and children good-bye, and taking from a drawer the photographs of those of his children who were not present and kissing them fervently. He mentioned his dream to his wife, who tried to convince him of the folly of giving credence to fears founded on dreams.

About two hours later Jennings in endeavoring to repair electrical connections on the up-town track of the Eighth Avenue line, was lying prostrate across the track near the One hundred and Fifty-fifth Street Station. He did not hear the approaching train, nor did the motorman see him and he was struck and ground to death in full view of the passengers who were on the station platform at the time. Jennings entered the employ of the company in a very unimportant capacity, but by studying nights managed to secure his appointment as an electrician.

—*New York Times*
May 25, 1904

Forewarned Of Accident
Wife Of Painter, Now Dead, Had
Premonition Of His Fate.

NEW YORK- Mrs. Jacob Miklowitz of 722 Columbus Avenue, whose husband was a boss painter had a premonition on Wednesday night, she says that her husband would meet with an accident. Miklowitz weighed 200 pounds. He and his younger brother Sigmund, were at work 85 feet up on the scaffold yesterday, when the wall cracked near one of the hooks supporting the scaffold and the scaffold fell. Sigmund caught a rope and was unhurt. His brother fell and was killed instantly.

—New York Times
August 4, 1904

The Spook Had Gone
Policeman Muldoon, Though, Found Out The Route He Took.

BROOKLYN- Policeman Muldoon of the Gates Avenue Court, Brooklyn, succeeded yesterday in getting Hugh Moore and his wife, Cora Moore, to court to answer the complaints of Mrs. Lauretia Sawtelle, Mrs. Ida Vitehn and Jacob Rasmussen, growing out of a lively "materializing séance" at the home of the Moores on Thursday night. He didn't catch the "Indian spirit," "Falling Water" who was directly responsible for all the trouble.

When Muldoon went to the home of the Moores, on Madison Street, on Monday night, to serve the warrant on "Falling Water" he was met by Mr. Moore. "I'm looking for Falling Water or Running Water or Fire Water, I don't know which," explained Muldoon. "You mean Falling Water, one of my spirit controls," said Moore, with dignity. "Hey," and taking off his helmet, Muldoon mopped his brow with his handkerchief.

"I say," repeated the medium, with patience, that Falling Water is a shade.

"Don't try to guy me," said Muldoon. "I ain't looking for no window curtain, I'm after Falling Water." Medium Moore looked sad but retained his patience. "Falling Water," he explained, "was an Indian chief. His spirit materializes here at times, but he is now on the other side of the river." A great light dawned upon Officer Muldoon. "Oh, I see," said he, with a knowing smile; he's skipped to Manhattan." Muldoon then satisfied himself by requesting the Moores to go to court.

—*New York Times*
October 12, 1904

Psychic Phenomena
Presbyterian Minister Gives Many Interesting Experiences And Opinions

NEW YORK- Before a large gathering of Presbyterian ministers yesterday, Rev. Isaac K. Funk read a paper on "Psychic Phenomena," giving many interesting experiences and opinions. After relating several incidents which seemed to partially substantiate the claim that spirits communicate with the living, the speaker said: "The Bible certainly teaches us that spirits do communicate with men. After much careful investigation, covering a number of years, I think I am within bounds in saying that nine-tenths of what passes as psychic phenomena is fraudulent. Of the remaining one-tenth, coincidence would explain some and telepathy and clairvoyance would explain some. It is the remainder of this one-tenth that deserves the deepest thought."

—*Dallas Morning News*
November 8, 1905

Knew Death Was At Hand
Lyons Woman Asked Children To Send For Physician

LYONS- Mrs. Daniel Frahar died at midnight last night following a sudden attack of heart disease. Yesterday afternoon she visited with a neighbor, was in good health and spirits and upon returning home started to build a fire.

She was suddenly taken ill and she rapped on the window to some children saying, "Send for the doctor, I believe I'm dying." Dr. James W. Putnam was called but was powerless to do anything. The deceased was born in Saratoga. Her husband and one sister survive.

—*Syracuse Post Standard*
March 17, 1906

His Premonition Leads To Finding Wife Dead
Long Island Officer, Fearing Mishap, Hurries Home And Discovers Woman Had Ended Her Life.

CORONA- Policeman Frank Neumann of the Flushing L.I. station had a premonition that something was wrong at his home in Corona early to-day, and as soon as he was relieved of his tour of patrol, without waiting to change his uniform, hastened to No. 14 Chestnut Street, where his wife and he lived alone. There he found his wife, Mrs. Sadie Neumann, dead, a gas tube at her lips, and about her mouth burns caused by carbolic acid. She had used both to make her death doubly sure.

The odor of gas reached the policeman before he succeeded in opening the front door. Not daring to strike a light he went at once to his wife's room, where he found her door locked. The keyhole was plugged. Frantically breaking the door, Neumann fell for the bed where he knew his wife must be dead or dying.

The gas tube extended from a chandelier overhead, and the woman had partly swallowed one end. Scars about her mouth betrayed the poison which she had taken, and it was evident that she had been dead for some time. Neumann declares that he is absolutely at a loss to account for his wife's act. They had had no disagreement of any kind and she had given no inclination that she had intended taking her life.

—*Syracuse Post Standard*
February 13, 1908

His Premonition Of Death May Come True

SYRACUSE- The condition of James Goldup whose wife died Saturday night is extremely low and his death is feared any moment. Some time ago Mr. Goldup met with an accident, receiving a dislocated hip and several fractured bones. He has never recovered from the injuries and his wife's death Saturday was a terrible shock to him. He then remarked that he would follow her within twenty four house. No hope is entertained of his recovery.

—*Syracuse Herald*
August 10, 1908

His Premonition Of Death Came True

SYRACUSE- James Goldup of No. 410 South West Street, true to his prediction of last Sunday night that he would soon follow his wife, who died at that time, to the grave, died at 9:30 o'clock last night. He was 73 years old. He suffered from a stroke of apoplexy Wednesday night, causing his death.

The shock from his wife's death was a strong contributory cause however. Surviving the husband are two daughters, Mrs. William H. Gadow and Mrs. Archie Urozier, and a son Alfred G. Goldup all of this city. Mr. Goldup's funeral will be held at 2:30 o'clock Monday afternoon.

—*Syracuse Daily Herald*
August 15, 1908

Mrs. Baker Had Strange Premonition Before Told Of Murder Of Her Brothers

SYRACUSE- After a strange premonition that "something dreadful was going to happen" Mrs. Libbie Baker of this city, sister of the Boil brothers who were murdered at Ingalls crossing Saturday night, was almost overcome when she received a telephone message summoning her to her home at No. 600 Park Street. She is employed at Blodgett's restaurant in South Clinton Street and all the week her nerves have been in bad condition because of a remarkable dream that came to her on three consecutive nights.

Only yesterday morning she told one of the girls in the restaurant:
"I have had a dream for three nights right along that blood was running down my face. I am afraid something dreadful is going to happen." This dream was so strange and its coming for three nights in succession so worked upon Mrs. Baker's nerves that it made her almost ill. When word came by telephone for her to go home she feared that some ill had befallen her son, Henry. She did not know till she reached home that anything was wrong with her brothers and then she was told only that they were sick and did not learn the true state of affairs until she reached Phoenix.

—*Syracuse Herald*
October 14, 1908

Her Dream Saves Children
Mother Kept Them From Going Driving Which Ended In A Runaway

BROOKLYN- Mrs. Kathleen O' Connor of 92 Marion Street, Brooklyn, said yesterday that she believed the lives of her two children were saved by a premonition she had in a dream of an accident which happened to her husband while driving a horse and buggy on Buffalo Avenue Brooklyn, Sunday afternoon.

According to his custom, John J. O'Connor, a liveryman, intended to take his two children, Eddie, 9 years old, and Daniel, 3, for a ride on Sunday. Mrs. O'Connor tried to dissuade him from taking the trip, declaring positively that she believed something would happen. She had a dream Saturday night she said, that an accident would befall him that day. She refused to allow the children to accompany their father, but he thought little of her fears, and drove off alone in his double seated carriage.

As O'Connor was crossing Herkimer Street he did not notice the approach of an automobile owned and driven by John Reineking of 376 Euclid Avenue and before either of the parties was aware of each other the auto struck the carriage. O'Connor was thrown to the street. The rear end of the carriage was smashed and broken off from the fore part of the carriage, and was caught a few blocks away by Policeman William Butler of the Atlantic Avenue Station. O'Connor

received severe bruises on the hand, head, and body, but was not hurt seriously. It was the part of the carriage that was wrecked which the O'Connor children always rode in.

—*New York Times*
January 5, 1909

Bride Found Dead; Gas On
Her Mother, Warned In A Dream, Met Son-in-law At Threshold Of Home.

NEW YORK- A husband of two weeks, returning from work for dinner yesterday with his bride in their furnished room at 199 Third Avenue, met the bride's mother on the stairway. The latter, though angered by her daughter's marriage, had dreamed that all was not well with the girl, and had come to see and forgive her.

Mother and son-in-law entered together and found the young wife dead in bed, with the gas flowing from a jet. The bride before her marriage was Miss. Ceila Talburg of 1167 Fox Street, the Bronx. She was a Roman Catholic, and Frank McDermott, the young bookkeeper who wooed her, was a Protestant. Because of this difference in faith the bride's mother and McDermott's family had objected bitterly to the marriage. Two weeks ago McDermott and the girl slipped away to New Jersey and were married. They took the room in the Third Avenue house.

A week ago Mrs. McDermott went to see

her mother, and, according to Mrs. Talburg, they quarreled. McDermott met a similar reception at his home, it is said, so the newlyweds determined to stay away. McDermott had no employment when he married, but he had saved a little money. They purchased a gas stove and set it up on a table, and, by attaching a rubber tube to a gas jet on the wall, were able to cook light meals. On Thursday McDermott got employment with the Trow Directory people and left yesterday for his first day's work. His wife, he says, was happy and kissed him good-bye. She gave no hint of a wish to die. At noon, McDermott went home and was astonished to meet his wife's mother on the stairs. "I dreamed last night there was something the matter with Celia," said Mrs. Talburg. "I was downtown shopping and decided to come and see her."

"Oh, she's all right," answered McDermott. "She was as happy as a bird this morning." They went upstairs together, and a little later were found by other tenants grief-stricken in the little room where the young wife lay dead. The gas tube was hanging suspended from the jet on the wall. There were no letters found to confirm the police report of suicide. McDermott says he believes his wife took the tube from the stove, but forgot to turn off the gas.

—*New York Times*
July 17, 1909

Finds Seal In Dream
New York Physician Had Lost It From Valuable Ring

NEW YORK- Dr. John T. Sprague, sanitary superintendent for the Department of Health for Richmond borough, is rejoicing over the recovery of a seal used as a setting to a ring, by means of a dream, almost before he knew he lost it. The seal was valuable because of its associations. It was used by a general in the Mexican war, and became the property later of Dr. Sprague's grandfather, then of his father and eventually came into Dr. Sprague's possession.

On Sunday night Dr. Sprague was awakened by a dream, in which he saw the stone lying in the street. He instinctually felt for the seal and found it was really missing from the ring. He then set about trying to recall the surroundings of the spot where he dreamed the stone was. After going over most of his movements of the day before, he hit upon a place in Water Street, Stapleton, near a drug store at 3 o'clock in the morning, and after much persuasion induced Mr. Colton to dress, take a light and search for the seal. Within ten feet of the spot indicated by the doctor over the telephone Mr. Colton found the stone.

—*Syracuse Herald*
September 5, 1909

CHAPTER 7 PSYCHIC PHENOMENA

EXTRA! EXTRA!

In 1900, the average life expectancy was 47 years.

Dead Brother's Spirit Message

**Woman In Italy Had Premonition Of Utica Murder.
The Night Children Were Slain She Had Strange Dream.
The Next Day She Mailed A Letter To Her Brother
Telling Of Her Dreams,
Before She Heard Of The Crime.
Psychologists Are Interested In The Story.**

UTICA- Considerable interest is being evidenced by the American Society for Physical Research in the remarkable dream of Mrs. Dominco Clanci, a sister of Ercole Infusino of this city, in which Mrs. Clanei who resides in Italy, claims to have had a premonition of the ravine tragedy on the night of September 13th when Theodore Rizzo, who was electrocuted last Monday at Auburn Prison, lured Theresa Procopio and Fanny and Fernando Infusino. To-day Dr. James H. Hystop of New York, secretary of the American Society for Physical Research, communicated with professional friends in this city, asking what means could be taken to protect the story of the dream from skepticism.

Dr. Hystop said that his desire to have the story corroborated was in the interest of science.

The two children were murdered by Rizzo on the night of September 12th. Fifteen days later Infusino, father of one of the slain children received a letter from his sister in Italy. Mrs. Dominco Clanci, who related a dream that she had on the night of September 12th, at about the same hour that the shooting is supposed to have taken place. In her letter Mrs. Clanci says that her brother, Thomas Infusino, who was killed in a sewer accident in West Utica May 7th 1897, appeared to her in the dream and told her she must go to America at once, where the children of Ercole were in great trouble and must be rescued. The spirit of the dead brother kept saying Mrs. Clanci declares, that Ercole's little children were out in the dark and cold and some one was seeking to them harm.

At the time Mrs. Clanci wrote this letter she had not heard of the murders, for the letter was mailed in Italy the following day, September 13th. She stated to her brother that the dream worried her a great deal and she wanted him to let her know as soon as possible if anything serious had happened.

After Mr. Infusino received the letter from his sister, little Fanny, the sole survivor of the tragedy, told her parents that the night of September 12th, while she was heroically keeping guard over her wounded brother a small dog appeared in the clump of golden rod where she was sitting and playfully licked her hand and also hand of Fernando as he lay dying. Mr. Infusino is positive that his sister in Italy had not heard of the tragedy when she wrote the letter in which she describes her dream. The crime was not discovered until the morning of September 13th, at about the time that Mrs. Clanci wrote the letter, and therefore he declared that even a cable message would not have reached her in time to enable her to "fake" such a story even if she had been disposed to do so. Whether Mrs. Clanci's dream constitutes a case of mental telepathy or a message from the spirit world is open for argument. At any rate it forms one of the most interesting cases of unexplainable coincidence that has come under the notice of psychologists.

—*Syracuse Herald*
November 28, 1909

Spirits Asked
To Aid Child
Occult Assistance Sought For
Daughter Of Professor Hyalop

NEW YORK- Although both Professor James Hyalop and Dr. Titus Bull, the two most interested, deny they have requested supernatural aid in the treatment of the former's young daughter, now (can't read) spiritualists and psychics throughout the city are lending every effort to gain occult assistance to bring about the girl's recovery.

Prayers have been offered in the hope of gaining the intercession of the hosts of another world to restore the child in health. The mystics are the more eager to work a miracle, since they are under the impression that Professor Hyalop and Dr. Bull are fully in sympathy with their precepts, whereas both are pronounced in their declaration they neither asked such help nor take steed in the teaching of the persons who have allied themselves with them.

At the home of Mrs. E. Monroe Hand, No. 324 West Seventy-sixth Street, during the regular meeting of the First Association of Spiritualists last Friday, Mrs. Hand announced to the hundred or more men and women there she had been asked to request the concerted prayers of all true believers for the welfare of Winfred Hyalop. She related the circumstances of the request in a detailed manner and gave several of her hearers the impression it had been contained in a request from Dr. Bull, who, with Dr. F. M. Crandell, is in charge of the patient. The alleged request, it was asserted, came direct from Mrs. Bull.

—*Syracuse Herald*
February 13, 1910

Writing Sermon On Comet

**Vision Reveals It To Him.
Rev. J. William Johnson Of Oneida
Tells Of Strange Experience
Following Prayer That He Might
See Star Before Preaching On It.**

ONEIDA- Rev. J. William Johnson relates an interesting experience with the Halley comet. He had prepared a sermon on the comet and had made it a subject of prayer that he might see the comet before the time came Sunday evening lest to deliver the sermon. Thursday night he performed a marriage ceremony and did not reach home until after midnight. About 3 o'clock he dreamed that a man was standing by his bed holding up a picture of the sky showing the location of the comet, and directing him to go to the southwest window and look towards the southwest, where he would see a yellow streak in the sky.

The vision was so vivid, said Mr. Johnson, that he awoke and going to the window, scanned the sky, finally discerning the comet. He retired only to be awakened again by the same vision. He awakened his wife and other persons in the house and then started to arouse the neighbors. In his sermon Sunday night and to many since, he related the story of his visions he had.

—*Syracuse Post Standard*
April 28, 1910

**EXTRA!
EXTRA!**

Oneida has the world's smallest church with the floor dimensions 51" x 81".

Had A Premonition Of Attempt To Kill

NEW YORK- A singular feature of the assault on the Mayor developed to-night when Mrs. Vingut told her mother having arisen early this morning at St. James and insisting that something was going to happen to her husband. The Mayor had stayed in town at the Hotel Manhattan over night.

Mrs. Gaynor, according to Mrs. Vingut, was so agitated that she called up the Mayor's office in this city several times to see if anything had happened. She was assured that nothing had happened, the last time this answer was sent being within a minute of the time he was shot. When she finally did get the news she said, "I knew it. I was sure something was going to happen. I felt it all the morning."

—*Syracuse Post Standard*
August 10, 1910

Heavy Cannonading Near Gardner's Bay

STONINGTON- All day heavy cannonading has been heard in the direction of Gardner's Bay. A messenger from Fisher's Island reports a mysterious light last evening in that vicinity.

—*New York Times*
December 17, 1861

A Meteoric Explosion
Heavenly Convulsions
Near North Adams

NORTH ADAMS- We yesterday noticed briefly the meteor which was observable in

this vicinity on Sunday morning last at six o'clock. The phenomenon seems to have been one of an extraordinary character—something attended with results quite unusual in meteoroid bodies. Whenever noticed it was accompanied by a low rumbling sound in the earth, and at Benihana people supposed that a repeated of Thursday's earthquake had occurred. The Saratoga describes its appearance near the village of Saratoga Springs.

Something is wrong "down below." Either the earth has got the core or is going to have it. Friday's quake was a bad symptom, but the thing seems to be not ended yet. Here comes Jefferson Ramsfelt, who resides on the east shore of Saratoga Lake, about three-quarters of a mile below Moon's and reports that early Sunday morning, before the sun was up, he being out doors at the time, his attention was arrested by a low deep rumbling sound as if from the very bowels of the earth. The noise had hardy ceased when she saw an immense meteor appearing as large as a man's hand, shouting swiftly across the firmament from north to south. Just as it reached the southern limit of vision it appeared to split up and divide into several parts. The noise and the melting was heard and seen by several persons beside Mr. Ramsfelt.

But the most remarkable phenomena connected with the meteor were seen at North Adams. Here the citizens were greatly alarmed and supposed from the rumbling and tremor of the earth that the glycerin works at Hoosac tunnel had been blown up. But it turned out from the observation of numbers of persons that the meteor burst in that vicinity, and that it was the cause of the commotion. The explosion shook the buildings and earth for miles around. Truly, with earthquakes and meteors, and gales and other phenomena, the year 1870 is one that cannot be sneezed at.

—*New York Herald*
October 27, 1870

❖❖❖

Portents In The Sky

NEW YORK- A white cross on the moon and a red sword in the northern sky on Monday night last excited the wonder of New Yorkers. In the minds of some they aroused fear. The sign sharps, those wise folk who profess intimacy with the occult, varied in their interpretations of the causes of the white cross and the red sword, but

all agree that they portend trouble for somebody.

The red sword is explained by the materialists, who scoff at signs and deny the possibility of wonders other than the wonders of law, as being due to a fire far up the shores of the Hudson and near the water. The river acted as a reflector to the flames. The explanation is not wholly satisfactory, however, because the fire sword remained steady and vertical for two hours. The white cross on the moon's countenance is certainly not accounted for by the fire theory. It was probably only a halo which, by a singular coincidence, broke into the form of a cross on the same night that the fire in Fort Lee caused the appearance of a flaming sword of war in the northern heavens. Ice crystals in the lower air through which the moon is seen are sufficient to account for the cross formation. But while a material basis for the two phenomena may be conceded, the sword and the cross, which have appeared so often in history side by side, may well have disturbed the minds and excited the imaginations of those who yet retain belief in the miraculous.

—*Syracuse Evening Herald*
March 10, 1898

A Brilliant Meteor
Shot Across The Southern Heavens, Last Night, Leaving A Track Of Light.
As Seen In Goshen.

GOSHEN- A meteor of dazzling brilliancy shot across the southern heavens about 10 o'clock. It seemed very near the earth, and all who saw it are agreed that it must have struck somewhere near here.

The population of Fulton Street, who as usual were nearly all out of doors, were badly frightened, and many of them declare to-day that the celestial visitor stopped right on that thoroughfare. The flight of the meteor was seen by only a few of our citizens, while others who only saw the trail of light that it made thought at first that it was a particularly lurid flask of lightning. The meteor was seen by people in Pine Bush, who thought it must have struck somewhere near this city.

Our Goshen Correspondent Says:
A singular disturbance in the "heavens" startled a number of persons who witnessed it, last night. It occurred shortly after 10 o'clock. Suddenly a bright light streamed forth from somewhere such as might have caused by a large signal rocket. Shortly thereafter there was a "bustification" of some sort at a great height, and away up yonder something shot across the night, leaving a glowing trail in its wake which lingered for at least a minute.
N.B. – The witnesses of this truly remarkable phenomenon were all temperate citizens, and men of unimpeachable veracity.

—*Middletown Daily Argus*
June 23, 1898

EXTRA! EXTRA!

Strange sightings continue in New York's skies as each year hundreds of UFOs are reported by residents.

Meteor Seen Near Geneva

**Accompanied By A Bright Light And Loud Noise.
Dropped In Seneca Lake.
Tremendous Explosion Heard After Sinking.
The Concussion Felt For Several Miles,
With Glass Broken In Windows.
Several Farmers Along The Lake Testify To The Phenomenon.**

GENEVA- The farmers west of this city and Earle's Station, near the lake shore, bring reports of a meteor which fell into the lake this morning about 5 o'clock. It was extremely light here this morning early and the first sign of anything extraordinary was noticed by Mr. Gifford, a farmer, when he saw the shadows of something moving. The ball of light was dazzling and considerably more intense than an arc light and appeared about six feet in diameter.

The meteor struck the water about a mile from shore and a second later there was a terrific explosion which was felt in the southern part of this city. The effect of the explosion was disastrous to windows in the vicinity of Earls, breaking seventeen panes of glass in one house.

The meteor was also seen by a farmer, Arthur Russell, on the east side of the lake, David Balker, a farmer on this side of the lake, also gives a like account of the appearance of the meteor and reports have been brought in from as far as ten miles west of Seneca Lake show as to the shock.

—*Syracuse Post Standard*
January 6, 1901

Dawn Broke Yellow

**Erstwhile Dull Gray Is Saffron Hued Through Strange Phenomena.
Many Reasons Given For It.
Opinion Is That It Was Caused By Dirt Particles Accumulating In The Atmosphere Through Lack Of Rain.
Some One's Yellow Streak And Perhaps The Yellow Peril Other Reasons Advanced.**

SYRACUSE- The customary dull gray dawn did not appear above the horizon when the stars sank to rest and the day first peeped out this morning. The erstwhile gray streaks of dawn presented themselves shimmering saffron hued variety, and early risers called to the other members of the family to get up and look at the yellow dawn.

The strange atmospheric phenomena agitated the populace of this neck of the woods this morning. When the light of day first broke, sky and air were a bright yellow, which grew lighter and thinner as the day passed, and toward noon the atmosphere had resumed its normal condition. The Herald office was plied with queries and the astronomer of the office put in a busy day. "Lens" attempted to snap shot the ozone so he could give a faithful cause, effect, and diagnosis, but failed dismally, and reporters talked by the yard to local astronomers, weather prophets, sky jacks and oldest inhabitants to secure an air and accurate account for the phenomena. However, none was found who would make a positive statement, and for once the whole tribe of 'em had to admit they were beaten.

Of course, some reasons were advanced. They were mostly in the nature of guesswork; some of the guesses seemed logical; some were numerous; some were ridiculous; a lot of them were awful bad. The most reasonable one appeared to be: The continued dry spell had permitted an accumulation of fine dust and dirt in the air. There had not been the rain to clarify the atmosphere nor the wind to carry the particles away: consequently they remain in the air and will do so until they are gradually forced into the earth under the rays of the sun. Three well-known Syracusans advanced the foregoing reason.

Forecaster Puzzled

Forecaster Morgan R. Sanford, who is in charge of the local weather station, admitted that the strange state of the atmosphere had him guessing. He said he could give no reason for it, there was no smoke reported in the air any nearer than Northern Michigan and he would not say what it could be.

Prof. E. D. Roe, Jr., an astronomer at Syracuse University, was also put to guessing. There was nothing within his knowledge of earth or sky which would produce a yellow atmosphere under normal conditions, he said, but he advanced as a cause that the continued dry weather had allowed an accumulation of dust particles in the air. This he thought, coming between the earth and the sun created a yellow hue. He said the lack of rain and wind to carry the dust away probably cause the haze.

A few people insisted that the haze came from the forest fires in Michigan. They thought that the wind had carried the smoke from the fire this distance, but Forecaster Sanford scouted this theory. He said there was no haze west of Buffalo and if the condition came from the West it would first be observed in the western cities. Another guess made was that the smoke had been carried down from the Adirondacks, but there have been no fires in that region to speak of, and it is difficult to imagine how smoke enough could come down from there to envelop the country between here and Rochester within which the yellow atmosphere was reported today.

A well known local clergyman ventured the opinion that the atmosphere had become surcharged with soot and smoke because of the dry weather. He said the heavier air currents above drove the particles to earth and created a mist over the atmosphere. When the day first broke there appeared to be a pall over the earth. The sky was cloudless, but the first hours of the morning were dark looking and rain was expected. As the day grew the extreme yellowness was noted and then people began to compare notes and comment on the peculiar color of the day. Almost every one took an umbrella or rain coat with them to work but found them unnecessary.

Political Speculation

"A yellow streak" some folks chose to call the day. "Must be Rafferty's soliloquized "Pat" McGlade. "Look's like McGlade's," commented Rafferty. There were a lot of other suggestions as to whose "streak" it might be. John Bedford said he knew whose it was, but he passed the name out to only a few of his intimate friends. "T'aint mine," said "Willie" Johns and "Jim" Dunbar told "Willie" in a most unkind way: "Haint big enough for yours, 'Willie.'" It was suggested that it might have came from Frisco where "Joe" Gans got his quietus from Battling Nelson yesterday.

"Vas ess das?" a North side German asked another. "I teenk it ess dem yeller peril which is by San Frensensco now dat's come," said the other. "Dem yeller peril is a disease yet. It comes end you get it and vott is on de inside come by de outside end

splits all over like," was explained. "Vouldn't it be nice if a broo'ry should caught it," observed the other. Only a few of the many reasons for the phenomena are given. Toward noon the sun appeared. It showed a bright red through the mist and many people took it for the moon, however, for at the present time the moon is under the earth, diametrically opposite to the sun and it is impossible to see it in the day time. The afternoon brightened up and the haze gradually disappeared.

—*Syracuse Herald*
September 10, 1908

Puzzled At Albany

ALBANY- The peculiar atmospheric conditions reported from Syracuse, Watertown and other state points exist here to-day. Col. William F. Fox, superintendent of State forests said that while he had received a number of telegrams advising him of small fires in the Adirondacks, they were not sufficient enough area to have caused the hazy conditions here. "Furthermore," said Colonel Fox, "the prevailing wind to-day is from the south. I cannot account for the peculiar haze here unless possibly there are forest fires in Pennsylvania.

—*Syracuse Herald*
September 10, 1908

Brilliant Displays

OLEAN- A curious coincidence did happen. At exactly 9:29 o'clock, the very minute almost, when the comet began to transit the suns surface, a brilliant aurora borealis was noticed in the northern sky. The great gleam of light flashed and glowed in the starry night. Then shot upward and then disappeared, only to reappear again, in a moment, more brilliantly beautiful than before. The display lasted for six minutes and then died away for good.

But in the opinion of Professor E. T. Borst, head of Yerkes' observatory, and of Professor E. E. Barnard, one of the greatest living authorities on comets, the aurora was in no way traceable to the comet or the passage of the earth through the tail of the comet. "Just a coincidence," said Dr. Frost, "and we have been having some very brilliant displays lately, but they have been missing for some nights past." Now they have reappeared, but our observations show us that there has been great spots on the sun to-day and these sun spots account for the aurora.

—*Olean Evening Times*
May 19, 1910

EXTRA! EXTRA!

In 1857, toilet paper was invented in New York City by Joseph Gayetty.

Air-Ship Was Seen From This City
Reputable Witnesses Swear They Observed The Evolution Of The Machine For At Least An Hour Last Evening

DUNKIRK- Several people report that an air ship passed over Dunkirk Thursday evening between six and seven o'clock, traveling in a westerly direction. Dennis

Ready, chief engineer at the city water works plants, says that he saw the aircraft for at least an hour, observing it through a telescope. A dozen others whose attention railed to the object in the sky saw the air ship.

Mr. Ready says that the airship consisted of two large cigar shaped gas bags one over the other and from the lower one was suspended a basket. He could not make out whether or not the basket carried any passengers. The air ship seemed to hang stationary about two miles off Point Gratiot and at once disappeared. Mr. Ready is of the opinion that it may have fallen into the lake.

—*Dunkirk Evening Observer*
September 23, 1910

INDEX
LISTED BY NEW YORK TOWNS

HIDDEN HEADLINES of NEW YORK

HIDDEN HEADLINES of NEW YORK

HIDDEN HEADLINES of NEW YORK

HIDDEN HEADLINES of NEW YORK

HIDDEN HEADLINES of NEW YORK

HIDDEN HEADLINES of NEW YORK

About the Author

Chad Lewis is a paranormal investigator for
Unexplained Research LLC, with a Master's Degree
in Applied Psychology from the University of
Wisconsin-Stout. Chad has spent years traveling the
globe researching ghosts, strange creatures, crop for-
mations, werewolves, and UFOs. Chad is a former
State Director for the Mutual UFO Network and has
worked with BLT Crop Circle Investigations. Chad
is the organizer of *The Unexplained* conferences
and the host of *The Unexplained* paranormal radio
talk show. He is the co-author of the *Road Guide to
Haunted Locations* series.

SOUTH DAKOTA
Road Guide to
Haunted Locations
by Chad Lewis & Terry Fisk
Foreword by
Michael Thomas Coffield

ISBN-13: 978-0-9762099-3-5

IOWA
Road Guide to
Haunted Locations
by Chad Lewis & Terry Fisk
Foreword by
Mike Whye

ISBN-13: 978-0-9762099-4-2

Credit Card Purchases Online at
www.unexplainedresearch.com

UNEXPLAINED RESEARCH
PO BOX 2173
EAU CLAIRE WI 54702-2173

The UNEXPLAINED Presents

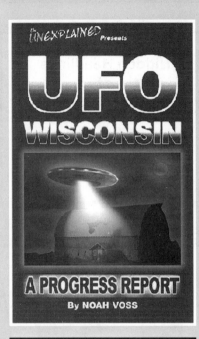
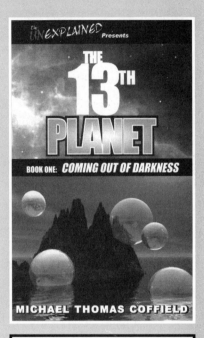

HIDDEN HEADLINES

Strange, Unusual, & Bizarre
Newspaper Stories 1860-1910

Hidden Headlines
of
WISCONSIN

Researched and Compiled by
Chad Lewis
Foreword by Michael Bie

ISBN-13: 978-0-9762099-6-6

Hidden Headlines
of
TEXAS

Researched and Compiled by
Chad Lewis
Foreword by Nick Redfern

ISBN-13: 978-0-9762099-8-0

Hidden Headlines
of
CALIFORNIA

Researched and Compiled by
Chad Lewis

ISBN-13: 978-0-9798822-0-3